REAL-WORLD INTELLIGENCE

Organized Information for Executives

Herbert E. Meyer

STORM KING PRESS
Friday Harbor, Washington

Storm King Press books are available at special discounts for
bulk purchases for sales, promotions, premiums, fund raising or
non-profit educational use. Special editions or book excerpts
can also be created to specifications. For details contact:

Storm King Press
P.O. Box 2089
Friday Harbor, WA 98250

Tel: (360) 378-3910

Fax: (360) 378-3912

Manufactured in the United States

ISBN 0-935166-05-X

For Jill, who gives me
the love and the elbow room
I need to make my way.

Also by Herbert E. Meyer

THE WAR AGAINST PROGRESS, 1979

HOW TO WRITE (co-authored with Jill M. Meyer), 1986

CONTENTS

BUSINESS INTELLIGENCE UPDATE

Books by former government officials fall into two general categories: those in which the ex-official writes about what he saw and heard—the so-called "Kiss-and-Tell" memoirs—and those in which the ex-official writes about what he learned. After resigning from the Reagan Administration at the end of 1985, after four years as Special Assistant to the Director of Central Intelligence and Vice Chairman of the CIA's National Intelligence Council, I set out to write a book in the latter category. *Real-World Intelligence* was the result. My objective was to pass along to the general public, and in particular to the business community, what I had learned about the principles and methodology of intelligence.

I wrote *Real-World Intelligence* with a considerable sense of urgency. By the end of the 1970s, thoughtful people throughout the business world—executives as well as business school professors and management gurus—had come to recognize that information itself was a powerful competitive advantage; that the future would belong to those companies which could most effectively harness information. Indeed, by the end of the 1970s books and articles about the growing importance of information were streaming off the printing presses.

While *what* to do was clear—harness the increasing flow of information, then use it to make better decisions—*how* to do it remained a mystery. Virtually all the published literature provided readers with an elaborate analysis of why information would become so important, then stopped short of showing how to actually get a handle on the stuff. The reason was obvious: no one knew. Among managers and executives actually responsible for corporate decisionmaking, the result was a great sense of frustration that came from being told where to go but not how to get there. Having written about the subject myself —I was *Fortune's* Soviet specialist during the 1970s, but management issues interested me and I wrote about them whenever I could—I understood the problem but had no better idea than anyone else about how to solve it.

SHORTCUT TO A SOLUTION

At this point my career took an unexpected turn. I thought the new course I was embarked upon would take me away from the search for a solution to harnessing business information. In fact, the new course put me on a direct line toward that solution. Shortly after the Reagan Administration took office the President's new Director of Central Intelligence, William J. Casey, asked that I come to Washington as his Special Assistant. It was an irresistible offer; a chance not only to become part of the Reagan Administration but to do so in a key position within the tightly-restricted, highly-classified world of intelligence. I accepted Mr. Casey's offer, moved from New York to Washington, plunged into the business of intelligence and —so I thought—walked away from the question of how companies could harness information to compete.

The substance of my work was absolutely fascinating. The Reagan Administration rejected the then-fashionable notion that the US-Soviet struggle was an eternal feature of life on earth; that the Cold War would go on forever with neither the Soviet Union nor the U.S. ever gaining the upper hand for long. Instead, the President believed that history was on our side, not on theirs, and that by unleashing America's economic and technological prowess and by deploying our most powerful weapon—the idea of freedom—we could, as the President so memorably put it, dump Communism into history's dustbin.

Our job at the CIA was to monitor the broad range of global issues that the President and his advisors needed to deal with as they struggled to change the course of events: Soviet strategic and military policies, Third World military insurgencies and political instabilities, European economic integration, Japan's economic juggernaut, the emergence of new technologies, shifting demographic patterns, and all the other geo-political issues so vital to our country's national security during the tumultuous, ultimately decisive 1980s.

Equally fascinating to me was the very process of intelligence work. It was the most orderly, intellectually rigorous process in which I had ever participated. First, starting with the Administration's goals as outlined by the President, we figured out what information he and his advisors would need; what information would be relevant to the strategic objectives they had set for the country. Then we went out and got it. Then we analyzed the information until we thought we understood its significance to the United States. In other words, we transformed raw information into intelligence. Finally, we prepared our reports and delivered them to the right officials at the right time to meet their decisionmaking needs.

In short order I realized that at the CIA, we were doing precisely what so many people in the business world were struggling to figure out how to do. We were harnessing information to compete. I felt like a scientist who unexpectedly finds something useful growing in a test tube and shouts "Eureka!" To my surprise I had "discovered" that the management tool business experts and executives were struggling to conceptualize and invent already existed. It was called "Intelligence." And while a very few companies had already figured it out—mostly in Asia and Europe, with just a few in the U.S., as outlined in the book itself —the vast majority of companies had never heard of intelligence or established a mechanism even remotely similar to this one.

REMEMBER THE WHIZ KIDS?

This wasn't the first time the U.S. Government had blazed the trail to a new management tool. During World War II, a group of smart young officers stationed at the Pentagon "discovered" that the Army had an orderly, highly efficient way of preparing for the future which it called strategic planning. These officers, who became known as the Whiz Kids, quickly realized that while some companies had already figured out a methodology for strategic planning the vast majority had not. The Whiz Kids recognized how useful and effective a management tool like this one would be in business, and they vowed to do something about it. After the war they set out to re-invent strategic planning as a business management tool.

The rest is history. After an initial phase of "What's that?", followed by a second phase of "Oh, yeah, I think we already do it", strategic planning became a widely understood, universally accepted business practice. Today virtually every company has a formal, established mechanism for setting objectives. Some companies do it all internally; others use outside experts. But today every chief executive understands the value of strategic planning and can describe the process by which his or her company formulates its own plan.

I set out to do precisely the same thing for intelligence. *Real-World Intelligence* was intended to help people in business to conceptualize the idea of intelligence as a management tool, and to give them a feel for what intelligence systems look like and how they work. My objective was to stimulate interest in, and generate enthusiasm for, the idea of intelligence. In a sense, *Real-World Intelligence* was designed to serve as a sort of booster rocket that would help blast the idea of business intelligence off the launch pad.

The "liftoff" phase took several years, lasting through the entire second half of the 1980s. Articles on the subject began to appear in cutting-edge business publications. The corporate conference and seminar circuits began to include business intelligence on their programs. More important, a growing number of companies began to take the idea of business intelligence on-board. Most of these companies that moved into business intelligence in the late 1980s focused narrowly, often exclusively, on competitor intelligence. Their usual approach was to select one or two staff analysts from somewhere in the bowels of the company and assign them responsibility for collecting and storing information about other companies in the same industry.

SECOND-STAGE IGNITION

But as we entered the 1990s business intelligence began to move forward at a much faster velocity. Today those of us in the business-intelligence business feel like astronauts after the spent booster stage of their rocket has dropped off and the second stage has ignited; we can almost feel ourselves being pressed back into our seats as the rocket accelerates and streaks upward. The "fuel" for this second-stage ignition of business intelligence is the high-octane mixture of history and technology.

The end of the Cold War turned both Eastern Europe and the Soviet Union into powerful magnets for Western companies. New opportunities for investment, especially in Eastern European countries where privatization of state-owned enterprises became a key part of economic recovery, created an enormous demand among Western executives for information they had never needed before: about economic and political developments in Hungary, Poland, Czechoslovakia and the other former Soviet satellites; about competitors' plans for investing in the region, and about potential funding sources including Western governments and government-supported banks. For companies eyeing the vast Soviet market, information about such highly political issues as relations between the central government in Moscow and the various Republic governments—in particular their struggle for control of the Soviet Union's industrial and natural resources—became matters of intense commercial interest.

Decisionmakers throughout the business world needed to know about these issues, and others triggered by the collapse of communism. They sensed the emergence of a new business order to match the new political order, and they came under enormous pressure to move swiftly or be left behind. What they needed most was information itself, so by necessity they became more receptive to the idea of a management tool that could filter out irrelevant information and deliver relevant information to the right executives at the right time.

The end of the Cold War also accelerated the trend toward globalization of business. Joint ventures and strategic alliances among American, European, and Japanese companies became the rage as the the big multinationals scrambled to position themselves for what they perceived to be the global marketplace of the 1990s. This too created a demand for new information—about markets, technologies, competitors' plans for competing internationally alone or as part of consortia—and a new receptivity among multinational executives to whatever methodology could monitor and deliver this kind of information swiftly, accurately, and efficiently.

At the same time, the end of the Cold War forced Western governments to re-think the role of their own intelligence services. In Washington, members of Congress as well as senior intelligence officials began to ask what role—if any —the CIA should play in a world where economic competition had replaced military competition as the driving force of global affairs; where trade negotiations were now perceived to be more important to national security than arms talks. One immediate by-product of shining the spotlight on intelligence was to illuminate the emphasis on analysis, and the corresponding de-emphasis on operations, that had already begun to take place even while the Cold War raged. This, in turn, revealed intelligence to be at heart an information gathering and monitoring process whose value to policymakers would be even greater in the less dangerous—but vastly more complex—post-Cold War world.

Meanwhile, in Europe and Asia government officials began to talk openly of using their countries' intelligence services to help local companies compete against foreign competitors. To be sure, some of these intelligence services had always engaged in this kind of clandestine activity. Indeed, the willingness of some European and Asian governments to use their intelligence services for commercial advantage against American multinationals had long been a sore point with U.S. officials who were aware of this activity, but who were blocked from doing anything about it by the overriding need to maintain good relations with our allies while the Soviet military threat took precedence.

But now this clandestine commercial intelligence activity began to come out into the open, and the nature and value of commercial intelligence became a public issue. Even the head of the Soviet Union's KGB chimed in. In what General Vladimir Kryuchkov apparently thought would be taken as a measure of his organization's post-Cold War moderation, he announced that henceforth the KGB's vast espionage apparatus would be available to help fledgling Soviet commercial enterprises to compete against their Western competitors. (Now, with the political collapse of the Soviet Union itself, it remains to be seen whether the KGB and other intelligence units of the old structure will survive to help industry in the various Republics to compete internationally.)

In short, the end of the Cold War put spotlights both on business *and* on intelligence. Very quickly the two began to overlap. Now there was not only a need, but a *recognition* of the need, for a management tool that any company could operate to harness the growing volume of available information and use that information to make better decisions.

THE NEW TECHNOLOGY

It was technology that made it possible to fully convert the idea of intelligence into a management tool. The technology for business intelligence is software. More precisely, it is information correlation software that not only reaches out and pulls in the vast amount of available information a company needs, but also sorts through this information to project patterns of activity.

The best way to explain how information correlation technology changes the very nature of the intelligence process is through an analogy:

During the early days of aviation a pilot would put on a pair of goggles, climb into the cockpit and fly by the seat of his (or her) pants. The trick was to keep your eyes peeled, and to hope you saw a looming danger before you flew into it. As airplanes got bigger, pilots had co-pilots on board to help out, and now two pairs of eyes were scanning the flight path looking for other airplanes, mountains, buildings, and storms. Later, with the advent of navigators, there were three pairs of eyes in the cockpit. But as airplanes got still bigger and faster—as they flew higher and further and as the volume of traffic increased—the danger grew exponentially of not seeing something until it was too late.

The solution was *not* to put still more pairs of eyes into the cockpit. For one thing, any airplane with a cockpit large enough to hold that many people probably couldn't get off the ground. Even if such an airplane could fly, managing all these people and keeping them from tripping over one another would be a nearly impossible job for the busy pilot. Most of all, no matter how many people could be jammed into the cockpit and no matter how well a pilot could manage them, the fact is that none of these lookouts would have better than 20/20 eyesight. Given the speed of the aircraft and the volume of traffic, 20/20 eyesight simply would not be good enough to assure safety.

The solution, of course, was radar. To the pilot, radar is a technology-driven management tool that scans the external environment through which the airplane is flying and projects patterns of activity. It enables the pilot to see clearly what is going on out there. Radar doesn't tell the pilot what to do; it merely lets him see things early enough to respond. The assumption of radar is that with the best possible information competent pilots will nearly always respond appropriately. Radar is not only smaller and cheaper than a bunch of people in the cockpit, all staring hard out the windows. It is a better system in the sense that it sees further and more broadly than humans can see, and in the sense that radar technology correlates the information it collects and projects patterns on a screen so the pilot can see it all clearly and at a glance. When radar became commercially available, each pilot chose the most appropriate model for his airplane and—literally—cut a hole in its instrument panel to make room for the new technological wonder. Before long radar systems were an integral part of avionics, and no sensible pilot would fly without radar on board.

RADAR FOR BUSINESS

Business intelligence is radar for business. What has happened during the last two years is that information correlation technology has combined with intelligence methodology. The offspring of this marriage is the business equivalent of radar: a fully integrated, turn-key Business Intelligence System that comes in a range of models suitable for any company of any size in any industry. These Systems can monitor information about a company's competitors, customers, suppliers, markets and about key trends in science, technology, economics and politics relevant to that company in light of its specific interests and objectives. Just as in the early days of radar, chief executives are now choosing the model best suited to the size and structure of their companies and, so to speak, retro-fitting this corporate radar into their instrument panels.

Like radar, a Business Intelligence System doesn't tell the executive—the pilot, as it were—what to do; it merely illuminates what is going on out there on the assumption that with good information a competent executive will nearly always respond appropriately.

Here I need to pause and outline my own role in the development and marketing of these Business Intelligence Systems. First, because the advent of these Systems has altered the course of business intelligence anyone seeking to understand the trajectory of this new management tool needs a grasp of what actually happened and how. Second, when I wrote *Real-World Intelligence* my hands-on experience was necessarily limited to government intelligence. Now I want to make clear that during the last few years I have had even more extensive, hands-on experience with business executives and companies using intelligence to compete. Thus the comments I will shortly make about some of today's executives and about the corporate cultures they have created—and about how these executives and cultures create obstacles to the effective use of intelligence in the business world—aren't the slightest bit theoretical. Rather, they flow directly from practical experience.

Very briefly, what happened is that in January 1989 I received a telephone call from Michael S. Pincus, chairman of Expansion Programs International, Inc. EPI, which is based in Cleveland and which operates under the trade name Thunderstone Software, had developed META-MORPH, which was and still is the world's most advanced information correlation software. Mike had just read *Real-World Intelligence* and, as he put it in that first telephone call, it was clear that while I had the methodology he had the technology. The obvious next step was to combine the two and create a system. This we did although, as with all inventions, it took more time, effort and money than either of us had anticipated. We formed a company—Real-World Intelligence Inc.—and like entrepreneurs everywhere we launched our product into the marketplace and started selling. As of this writing we have installed Business Intelligence Systems for companies in a wide range of industries including consumer products, aerospace, insurance, agri-business and pharmaceuticals.

OLD HABITS DIE HARD

The introduction of intelligence to companies is turning out to be trickier than we had anticipated. More precisely, in several instances we have found ourselves struggling with executives who were eager to get an intelligence system—they loved the *idea* of it and practically broke down our door to buy one—but unwilling to actually take advantage of the intelligence their system began to generate. It was rather like selling a radar only to discover afterward that the pilot never looked at the screen, preferring instead to keep to the old habit of flying by the seat of his pants.

While no two of our experiences have been precisely the same, at every company where we have encountered resistance to intelligence we have found the same three conditions:

—An inability among executives to see the underlying patterns that intelligence revealed, and thus a failure to grasp the implications of these patterns for their company;

—An obsession with what competitors are doing, to the point where executives ignore key trends and developments that affect their entire industry;

—The very culture of the company, specifically a frenetic, ad hoc, disorderly approach to doing business.

With time—and with training programs our company has, by necessity, developed—we have usually managed to overcome these conditions and get the company's executives to take full advantage of their intelligence system. Note that I say usually, which is not the same thing as always. In a couple of instances we literally had to give up, and come away from a company with the queasy feeling that its pilots just weren't going to use their radar. (In one of these instances the company did indeed crash some months later; according to reports in the financial press, experts sifting through the wreckage attributed the catastrophe, at least in part, to a lack of good intelligence.)

In looking back over the original text of *Real-World Intelligence,* I am relieved to find that I did in fact raise and discuss all three conditions. However, experience makes clear that I failed to highlight them sufficiently, and to alert readers that for a company to make effective use of the intelligence it acquires it is crucial to overcome each of these conditions, if they exist. Thus I want to expand on them somewhat in this update, as follows:

PATTERNS AND IMPLICATIONS

Think back for a moment to my earlier analogy of intelligence to radar. When a pilot glances at his radar screen he sees the current location, in relation to his own aircraft, of other airplanes. As he monitors his radar he will see the direction in which these planes are flying, and get a fairly accurate reading of their speeds. In other words, he will see a pattern of activity. And he will interpret this pattern in a way that enables him to grasp its implications for his own aircraft. For example, the pilot might see that all other aircraft are flying on courses and at speeds that will cause him no concern. Or, he might see that he is on a collision course with another airplane, and that based on the pattern of activity the two aircraft will collide in three minutes. At this point the pilot must decide what to do: slow down, speed up, change course, or whatever. Different pilots might choose different options but, at least in principle, all competent pilots will choose an appropriate *response based on the pattern of activity and on its implications as perceived by the pilot.*

Now let us take a business intelligence example: A company in the beverage business would be monitoring, among other things, new consumer-product trends. One day the System reports that in the breakfast cereals industry, "gender-specific" cereals—cereals designed and marketed to appeal specifically to either men or women—are becoming hot. One month later the System reports that Japanese automakers are shifting their marketing strategies to sell selected car models specifically to women. Two weeks after that the System notes that a European soap manufacturer which had begun to market two kinds of bath-sized bars—one to men and the other to women—is reporting sharply higher earnings. The pattern that emerges is clear: "gender-specific" products are flourishing.

But what does all this mean to our beverage company? That it should make both kinds of breakfast cereals available in the company cafeteria? That it should provide different company cars to its women sales reps? *Or does the intelligence suggest that the company start to market —or at least consider the idea of marketing—some kind of "gender-specific" beverage, for example a soft drink aimed specifically at women?*

This is what I mean by seeing the pattern and grasping its specific implication for a company. And this is what we find so many executives have trouble doing. They tend to become so caught up in the flow of information that they fail to use this information—to convert it into operational intelligence—by figuring out what dangers or opportunities the information presents to their company. It would be like a pilot who becomes so absorbed in watching all the activity on his radar screen that he never gets around to saying, Hey guys, we're on a collision course with that 747 jumbo jet off our port wing so let's come up with a response real fast.

The key to success in today's business environment lies in spotting a pattern with the fewest possible facts—before it is too late to respond and before the pattern is so obvious that your competitors catch on. Intelligence is the best tool for doing this on a regular, sustained basis. But it is only a tool, for there is no such thing as a computer that thinks or a "brain-in-a-box" that can make decisions for human beings. It is the human being—in this case, the corporate intelligence chief whose role is outlined in the text of *Real-World Intelligence*—who must use the tool effectively. He or she not only must monitor the flow of information but also keep asking: So what? What does this mean for us? What dangers or opportunities does this information illuminate? In light of our strategic objectives, what are the logical options?

THE COMPETITION AND THE TOTAL ENVIRONMENT

I cannot say it often enough: Knowing what your

competitors are doing is vital, but it is not sufficient. First, your competitors are moving through the same murky environment that you are moving through. The trick is to grasp the external conditions through which *all* of you are moving: the emergence of new technologies, shifting demographic patterns, changes in consumer spending and lifestyle trends, political upheavals, the opening of new markets, the broad range of government policies at home and abroad that impact business including budgets, taxes, regulations and the environment. These are the forces that shape events; that put new dangers—and opportunities—in your path. If the only thing you watch is your competitors, by definition you are condemned to react to whatever they do, rather than to lead and have them react to you.

Second, in today's environment the company that is most likely to do you damage isn't one of your competitors at all. More likely it is a company outside your industry armed with a new technology, or a new idea, that will profoundly change your industry—your company as well as your competitors. What did in the typewriter manufacturers wasn't another typewriter manufacturer, but the emergence of personal computers for word processing along with an entirely new industry to manufacture and market PCs. What threw the tin can makers for a loop wasn't a better tin can but the now-famous "drink-box" that stores easily on shelves and in children's lunch boxes and has a little straw attached that you poke through the top. The telegraph companies were done in by the fax. In today's environment being knocked off by a new company with a new technology, rather than by a traditional competitor, is becoming the rule rather than the exception. Once again, if all you do is watch your competitors, you are heading for a serious fall.

Having said all this, let me quickly acknowledge that you will go belly-up even faster if you focus so heavily on

Big Trends that you ignore your competitors. Of course you must monitor their strategies, their plans for new products, their financial health, their activities regarding joint ventures, strategic alliances, mergers or acquisitions. You need to know about changes in your competitors' earnings, their compensation schedules, even changes in their investment bankers and advertising agencies. You need to know who your competitors' key executives are and when they shift around within the company. You need to know your competitors' perceptions of the marketplace, which will enable you to better project whether your competitors plan to move forward aggressively or hunker down to merely survive.

The key point here is that competitor intelligence is only a subset of Business Intelligence. A good intelligence system will generate information about *all* the subjects and issues a company needs to monitor; about its competitors and about broad trends that affect the entire industry. But no system can automatically force executives to pay equal attention to both categories. You can see the danger: it is like a pilot who uses his radar only to monitor other aircraft—and then flies directly into a mountain. In today's business world, too many executives are so obsessed by what their competitors are doing that they ignore everything else. And there is no way to prove to them that their narrow focus is dangerous; it's a matter of common sense. Nevertheless, the habit of focusing on competitors to the exclusion of everything else is so strong, so deeply ingrained in business lore and practice, that the effort required to break this habit is enormous. But it must be done. As a practical matter, I would settle for moving a company that focuses 98 percent on its competitors to focusing just 75 percent on them. A shift of even this small a magnitude would make an enormous difference in a company's perception of its environment.

THE CULTURE OF CORPORATE DISORDER

I said earlier that intelligence is an orderly, intellectually rigorous process. Indeed, the description of this process and the explanation of how it works lies at the heart of *Real-World Intelligence*.

But today at too many large companies the culture is at odds with anything orderly and intellectually rigorous. Projects are started, re-directed, then canceled almost at whim. Managers are hired, shifted, dismissed. Corporate initiatives are announced, launched with fanfare, abandoned quietly over a holiday weekend. Last year's great strategic acquisition becomes this year's brilliant divestiture. Executives themselves are busier and busier, somehow accomplishing less and less. They have telephones in their pockets, faxes in their homes, schedules tightly packed with meetings that drone on forever and finally end without anyone having a clear idea of what, if anything, has been decided. The daily flow of events is frantic, frenetic, episodic, ad hoc, sometimes feckless and even random.

The chances of successfully introducing an intelligence system into this kind of madcap milieu are roughly equal to the chances of successfully imposing *Roberts' Rules of Order* on a bunch of seven-year-olds opening presents at a birthday party. The problem isn't producing intelligence, since in any organization one can usually find at least a few people who work in an orderly fashion and who can be trained as intelligence officers. The problem lies with the consumers; the decisionmakers to whom intelligence is delivered and who must use the intelligence as a guide to action.

Disorderly executives do not sit still long enough— physically as well as intellectually—to absorb a steady flow of intelligence and to use this intelligence effectively. They cannot remember what the intelligence told them last time, and lack sufficient patience to listen when it is explained to them. They cannot focus sharply enough to pick up on key new developments or even to frame a probing question. They live utterly in the present; what is past is forgotten and what lies ahead is of no interest. They are content to react rather than to act, and they equate good management with responding to events rather than to shaping events.

Introduce intelligence to an organization managed by executives like these and you are lighting the fuse for an explosion. For intelligence, more than any other process, reveals the true nature of an organization. It will make an orderly company look more orderly. And it will make a disorderly company look chaotic. By doing so it will deeply offend those executives who are responsible for the company's style and culture. For it will expose them as the incompetent clowns they are. Do not expect them to respond by changing; this isn't how incompetent executives respond when their incompetence is exposed. Rather, they will respond by cutting off—brutally—the process that reveals the truth about them.

Thus the failure of intelligence to take hold at a company can itself be an important piece of intelligence; it often indicates an underlying corporate disorder. Today this sense of disorder afflicts a large number of famous old companies. Many of them have already disintegrated, and in the years to come many more will go belly-up. Is a lack of intelligence among the causes of their impending collapse? Yes. Would the introduction of an intelligence System save them? Probably not, for the executives responsible for running these companies into the ground would reject intelligence as, no doubt, they are rejecting every competent manager with a good idea. (Intelligence

Tip: As you monitor your competitors keep an eye on the career tracks of their best managers. If these managers prosper, it is an indicator that your competitor is intellectually healthy and therefore likely to prosper commercially. If these managers are treated badly, it is a key indicator that your competitor is brain dead; flailing around, rudderless, likely to somehow set itself on a course toward self-destruction.)

A NEW BUSINESS PARADIGM

I keep describing business intelligence as a management tool. And so it is. But business intelligence is also something more, and it is this additional feature that makes its advent so important. Business intelligence is a reflection of a wholly new paradigm now emerging in our concept of ourselves and our universe; a fundamental shift in the way people operate and perceive which has come about as the result of new knowledge and technology. The clearest articulation of this paradigm shift that I know of comes from J. David Bolter, in his book entitled *Turing's Man*. Alan Turing was the British mathematician who, in the 1930s and 1940s, wrote the theoretical papers on which today's computers are based; in 1936 Turing's paper, *On Computable Numbers*, set out the nature and limitations of logic machines before a single fully programmable computer had ever been built.

Professor Bolter's thesis is that in the ancient world the drop spindle and the potter's wheel were the "defining technologies," and we saw ourselves through the paradigm of rotary motion and of human or animal power. From this perception came support for the ideas of the rotating universe, the animate nature of the stars, Aristotle's theory of form and matter. Bolter calls this paradigm of ourselves and our universe "Aristotelian Man." Centuries later, during the Renaissance, European philosophers found the clock and, later, the steam engine more suggestive than the manual crafts. They spoke of a clockwork world in which even animals and humans were intricately regulated machines. They viewed the world itself as a gigantic, incredibly complex clockwork. Bolter calls those who held this perception of man's relationship to his world "Cartesian Man," after the French philosopher Rene Descartes.

Today the personal computer is our "defining technology." In Professor Bolter's paradigm we are now "Turing's Man," in the sense that we see ourselves as "information processors" and the world around us as "information to be processed."

This suggests that a new kind of executive is emerging; one who recognizes that in today's world the business environment is comprised fundamentally of information, and that the ability to process this information is itself a key management skill. These are the executives who are most likely to learn and use the skills and techniques of business intelligence. They are also the ones most likely to be frustrated by the culture of disorder that prevails at so many large companies. If they cannot change this culture they will leave and launch ventures on their own. And to the extent that these new ventures make more effective use of information than do the larger companies, they will have an important, increasingly decisive strategic edge. This, in turn, will accelerate the re-structuring of industry itself, from a structure dominated by large companies to one in which power is more diffuse, resting with the smaller but vastly more energetic companies that can see opportunities sooner and move more swiftly to take advantage of them.

KNOWLEDGE, POWER, AND INTELLIGENCE

This diffusion of corporate power may well prove to be irreversible, for it rests on a fundamentally new relationship between knowledge, power and intelligence. The older view was articulated best by Francis Bacon, the great English statesman and philosopher who coined the phrase "Knowledge is power." Bacon also wrote that "We cannot command nature except by obeying her." Bacon's point is that the only way to control the forces at work in our world is to understand them. It is this *knowledge* of how the world works that provides the *power* to shape the future rather than be at the mercy of it. My partner, Michael Pincus, articulates the new perception: "Information is not, by itself, knowledge. Knowledge is *correlated* information, which is information filtered and selected to reveal an underlying pattern. Intelligence is knowledge used to accomplish a strategic goal. Power, then, flows from the effective use of intelligence."

For too long now, it has been acceptable in business to wait until the last possible moment before taking action—to wait until the danger is acute or until a new opportunity is so obvious that everyone can see it. We have taken to thinking of a good executive as one who has "lightning" professional reflexes. It is this perception which is now changing, and which must now change. For to compete effectively in today's fast-paced, complex, global business environment, "lightning" professional reflexes, while always nice to have, simply are not sufficient.

Increasingly, we are coming to recognize the power and value of professional *insight*—the ability of a manager or executive to see a looming danger or a new opportunity at the earliest possible moment, in plenty of time to make the necessary course correction. With insight, the need for "lightning" reflexes diminishes. More and more, we will come to understand that those who rely on "lightning" professional reflexes are condemned to react to decisions made by those of their competitors who have the advantage of professional insight.

Intelligence is the key. As technology continues to enhance our ability to harness information, insight will become available to any company or enterprise that wants it; whose executives have the skill, the energy and, most important of all, the intellectual courage to see the future clearly enough to shape it rather than be at the mercy of a future shaped by others. More and more in business, the power and prestige of leadership—in other words, the rewards of success—will rest with those executives who prove themselves most willing to take up the tool of intelligence, and to use the insights that intelligence provides as their chief guide to action.

Herbert E. Meyer
Friday Harbor, Washington
September 1991

REAL-WORLD INTELLIGENCE

CHAPTER ONE

THE MOST POWERFUL MANAGEMENT TOOL OF ALL

You ought to know that intelligence is the most powerful means to undertake brave designs, and to avoid great ruines: and it is the chiefest foundation upon which all generals do ground their actions.

—GENERAL GEORGE MONK,
*Observations Upon Military
and Political Affairs* (1671).

THERE is magic in the word "intelligence." Say it, write it, or think it, and you conjure up the most vivid images of danger, romance, and intrigue: spies meeting at a seedy restaurant in Berlin or in the shadow of a streetlight in Budapest; satellites streaking through outer space while peering down on enemy missile bases; car chases through the streets of Hong Kong, Mexico City, or Macao; gentlemen whose suit jackets are tailored to hide the bulge of pistols and whose briefcases will explode if improperly opened; impossibly beautiful women who do the most extraordinary things for their countries—not always while fully clothed; secret agents reporting in to CIA headquarters in Langley, Virginia, or to "the Circus" in London, or to Moscow's Dzerzhinsky Square; even the occasional body thrown from a speeding train.

No one likes to burst a balloon—especially this one, which is so much fun to play with. But in the real world, intelligence no longer bears much resemblance to these images, however vivid they may be. In fact, intelligence has become a far more interesting and exciting game than stealing somebody else's secrets ever was or could be.

What's happened is this: Within the community of intelligence professionals a realization has taken hold that to achieve your objectives in a fast-paced, multinational, information-driven world like ours you need to know more than just your adversaries' secrets. You need to know as much as possible about what's going on—and what's likely to go on—throughout the total environment in which you *and* your adversaries are operating. Science, technology, economics, politics—these are the forces that drive events. These are the forces that, together, shape the world in which you and your adversaries compete for advantage. Seeing these forces clearly is not easy; in a sense, it is very dark out there.

No longer does the leading edge automatically go to whichever competitor has the most raw strength. It can also go, and increasingly does, to whichever competitor has the best vision—the better grasp of what the key trends and developments are, and of how these trends and developments are affecting and will affect *all* the competitors. Of course you want to know your adversaries' secrets. But in today's world, access to secrets simply is not good enough. It's nice but not sufficient. You need much, much more. And these additional needs have changed the nature, the thrust, the very definition of intelligence.

> In the real world, intelligence has broadened to become organized information. More precisely, intelligence has come to mean information that not only has been selected and collected, but also analyzed, evaluated, and distributed to meet the unique policymaking needs of one particular enterprise. It is this transformation of what has been collected into finished, polished, forward-looking analytic products designed to meet the unique policymaking needs of one enterprise—and the organizational effort required to do it—that marks the difference between what intelligence used to be and what it has become.

You need only look within the world's best intelligence services to see how much the intelligence game has changed. No longer do these services have the look and feel of cloak-and-dagger operations that collect facts at whatever cost, wipe off the blood when necessary, and then pass on what they have collected to policymakers. Today these intelligence services resemble nothing so much as on-board ship or airplane navigation systems. Once the policymakers' orders for where the enterprise itself should head have been given, the service's first responsibility is to make sure that their policymakers know precisely where the enterprise is at any given time, no matter how bad the visibility. Second, the service is responsible for spotting whatever dangers and opportunities lie ahead—and for sounding an alert—long before these dangers and opportunities become apparent, and in plenty of time for the policymakers to take whatever evasive or aggressive action they judge to be appropriate.

In short, intelligence has become a management tool. Indeed, in the hands of policymakers who know where they want to go—whose strategic planning units have outlined a clear set of objectives—intelligence has become a tool of awesome power and flexibility. With access to "organized information"—to modern, real-world intelligence—the managers of any kind of enterprise can see what's going on out there right now, and more important, they can see what is likely to go on out there in the hours, days, weeks, months, and even years to come. Foreknowledge of this sort does not guarantee success, but it increases the chances of success—and you cannot ask for more than that.

Governments have been quick to understand the changed nature of intelligence. Today in virtually all of the world's best intelligence services, the heavy action has shifted from the operational side of the house to the analytic side. Intelligence budgets are always closely guarded secrets. But it is not a secret that in just about every country these budgets are rising sharply. And neither is it a secret that in most of these countries, most of the extra money is being used to beef up and expand these services' analytic capabilities. You need only come close to the upper echelons of policymaking to see that government leaders are increasingly basing their major foreign policy decisions and initiatives on intelligence "estimates" and other analytic products. This is true not only here in the United States but throughout the world.

Now businesses are beginning to catch on. Throughout the world of commerce and industry, "intelligence" is on its way to becoming a key management tool for corporate chief executives and their top policymaking lieutenants. Indeed, the development of "business intelligence" and the subsequent emergence of "business intelligence systems" is the most striking and potentially most important business trend of our time.

> For intelligence is nothing less than the crucial second half of strategic planning. It is the mechanism which enables a company that has a good strategic plan to chart and pursue a course that will bring the company to its objectives in the shortest possible time, no matter how rapidly or radically external conditions may change. And when external conditions change so radically that the plan itself needs to be altered, it is intelligence that sounds the first alert for the strategic planners themselves.

To be sure, successful business enterprises have been collecting and using intelligence in an organized manner since the late fourteenth century, when the House of Fugger—which from its base in Augsburg, Germany, made a fortune in textiles and mining, and then became one of the Continent's first international banking houses—launched its so-called "manuscript newsletters" to provide key officers with a steady flow of carefully selected political and commercial information. Since then, just about every business enterprise has developed some form of intelligence-collecting activity. Today most large companies have several intelligence-type activities under way, including market research, economic forecasting, political risk analysis, and a range of technologically oriented activities, such as the regular acquisition of competitors' new products for the purpose of taking them apart and "reverse engineering" the products to figure out how they were made.

It is this broadening of the concept of intelligence—from stealing secrets, which is legitimate for a government to do under certain circumstances but never for a private enterprise, to "organized information"—that has freed business to leap forward in the use of intelligence. Today the majority of large multinational companies regularly purchase intelligence analyses from one or another of the intelligence-consulting firms that have set up shop in the last few years. Based in the world's political and financial capitals—Washington, New York, London, Paris, Zurich, Tokyo—most of these firms are owned and operated by former high-level government officials who, in effect, are repackaging and selling to corporate clients, often for astoundingly huge fees, the information and insights they acquired while in office. With the support of topflight research teams—themselves consisting mainly of lower-level ex-government officials—these firms now provide intelligence to corporate clients at a level, and on a range of subjects and issues, never before available on the open market.

Within a small but growing number of companies, all the scattered and often unconnected intelligence-type activities already under way now are being pulled together into tightly organized—or at least coordinated—corporate units. And at a few trend-setting companies here in the United States, as well as in Europe and Asia, executives are actually working to install custom-designed business intelligence systems or to expand embryonic systems already in operation.

It is this new effort within the corporate community to acquire, organize, and coordinate the diverse elements of intelligence that is turning a group of related but previously separate activities into a wholly new—and incredibly powerful—business management tool.

In short, intelligence is becoming big stuff. So it is high time to erase the popular but wrongheaded images of intelligence and to draw an accurate picture. It is time to get a firm grip on what intelligence really is, why its use has become so widespread and so vital, and above all, how an intelligence outfit—a government calls it a service and a corporation calls it a system, but it's the same thing—really works.

Two warnings before we begin: First, despite my having some years of experience as a senior manager of our country's intelligence service, and then as a designer of business intelligence systems, what follows is not a kind of kiss-and-tell memoir. U.S. government intelligence is controlled by a complex pattern of security classifications—and rightly so. And the rules of confidentiality limit disclosure for business intelligence as well. Of course I will use as many genuine examples as possible. And since the principles of intelligence are the same for government and business, I'll use parallel examples most of the time to show how an intelligence outfit serves its policymakers regardless of whether the decisions are political or commercial. Where genuine examples cannot be used, I'll make the point with realistic but hypothetical examples.

So if you are hoping to learn some secrets here—some dirt on how the CIA goofed in one or another country, or on how some company really did in its competitors—you're reading the wrong book. It is illegal and unethical to give genuine examples of intelligence—and also very stupid. However, as you will see, it is not necessary to spill secrets to talk seriously about intelligence. Indeed, secrets can be so titillating and so distracting that spilling them often stops a serious discussion of intelligence dead in its tracks.

Second, be warned that if you read on for just a few more pages you will never again be able to think about intelligence the way you have been thinking about it until now. So if you have grown too fond of the racy and romantic images this word conjures up to tolerate a change, perhaps you had better shut this book now.

On the other hand, if you are responsible for managing a major enterprise such as a government or multimillion-dollar business, or if you have hopes of one day managing such an enterprise, the following pages will change the way you think and work. American business executives, in particular, take note: At a time when our country is scrambling to become as internationally competitive as possible, a grasp of how to use intelligence as a management tool can make all the difference to the fate of your company or enterprise. At the very least you will be able to even up the odds, since so many foreign companies right now use intelligence as a management tool far more extensively, and effectively, than does the U.S. business community.

So read on. You will learn what intelligence really is, how intelligence outfits really work, and above all, how *you* can use intelligence as a management tool to achieve your key objectives.

CHAPTER TWO

THE NEW INTELLIGENCE

It is pardonable to be defeated, but never to be surprised.

—FREDERICK THE GREAT

To grasp the concept of intelligence as organized information, you need only consider the difference between information and intelligence. Indeed, when you compare the two not only does the difference between information and intelligence become clear, but you can also see why access to intelligence has become so vital for effective decision-making by any government or business enterprise competing for advantage in today's world.

The best way to illustrate this difference between information and intelligence is to take a couple of examples that are realistic but (at least as of this writing) hypothetical:

First, imagine that the television program you are watching is interrupted by a news bulletin: RIOTS BREAK OUT IN EAST GERMANY. The reporter goes on to say that Potsdam and Leipzig have been sealed off to outsiders; that telephone lines have been cut; that there are unconfirmed reports of two dozen casualties; that the Soviet Union has said nothing but it is expected that the Russians will react swiftly and harshly to bring the situation under control.

Now, this is information—a report of the raw, basic facts as they are understood at the time. No doubt more facts will become available in the immediate future, and presumably, when they do, these additional facts will also be passed along in the same raw, basic form. For most people this flow of raw information is all that is needed. After all, rioting in East Germany, however surprising or interesting or appalling or heartening, is unlikely to have a direct impact on their own jobs or even their own organizations.

But for a few people, the outbreak of riots in East Germany will have a very direct impact. These are the people who need more than information. They need intelligence. Let's pick a few of these people and consider what their intelligence outfits would report to them (again, hypothetically) in addition to the information itself:

The Prime Minister of France:

The rioting in East Germany will undoubtedly be brought under control by the Soviets, either with their own troops or with East German troops under Soviet command and control. An emergency meeting of the NATO ambassadors has already been scheduled for 1 P.M. this afternoon in Brussels, and we expect heavy pressure to join in a statement condemning the East German regime. We also expect that NATO forces will be put on alert, but we believe this will be more for public appearances than out of genuine concern that the Warsaw Pact will use the rioting as an excuse to launch a military attack against the West. We see no danger to French interests, provided the situation comes under control quickly, as we believe is likely.

The President of the United States:

We have early indications that the rioting will spread to several other East German cities. In Moscow, the Soviet leadership is apparently meeting this morning, and we expect to have some evidence of troop movements by late this afternoon. The NATO draft communiqué has already been circulated and should be approved easily;

we don't yet know how the French will respond. You should anticipate an urgent request from the Chancellor of West Germany to avoid incendiary rhetoric of any sort; the West Germans are worried that the U.S. will inadvertently encourage the rioters and force the Soviets to invade East Germany, which the West Germans would quite properly view as catastrophic to their interests.

As yet, we see no evidence of broad public support for the East German rioters. But if the Soviets and East Germans overreact and use excess force, we might well see the rise of a Solidarity-type movement. Moreover, if such a movement takes hold in East Germany it could well trigger the rise of a parallel movement in Hungary or Czechoslovakia. It is this possibility that worries Moscow the most.

The Foreign Minister of Thailand, Who Is in Washington to Discuss Other Matters and Is Scheduled to Meet the President at 11 A.M.:

The President and his National Security Council will be preoccupied today with the crisis in East Germany. While we expect them to go forward with our 11 A.M. meeting, we must anticipate that the meeting will be shortened, perhaps to half an hour from the one hour we have been promised. The State Department undoubtedly will offer you a briefing on the situation and would look kindly on a public statement by you condemning the East German Communist regime. We believe you should anticipate an informal request by State to postpone your planned request for a change in U.S. tariffs to permit more Thai textiles into the United States. In sum we believe the Americans will be too distracted to deal seriously with this issue today, despite its great importance to our country.

The Chairman of Eagle Industries, an Ohio-Based Manufacturer of Heavy Machinery:

This mess in East Germany could throw a monkey wrench into our deal with the East Germans. As you know, we're in the final stages of negotiating a $7 million contract for export of our new pumps, which the East Germans want for their natural gas lines. Up to now Washington has made clear that we'll get the necessary export licenses. But now it's possible that the United States will put economic sanctions on East Germany, and our license application could get caught in the squeeze. Our people are scrambling to get formal approval of our export license before any sanctions can be announced; they are flying to Washington this morning for a meeting at the Commerce Department late this afternoon.

Since we're hoping to use this contract as a wedge to open up the East European market for our pumps, losing the deal now would cost us more than just the value of this contract. No doubt our English and West German competitors would be more than willing to supply the pumps if we're forced to drop out. Thus they would have the best shot at the entire East European market.

The Managing Director of Briggs-Hanson, a Wall Street Brokerage House:

The price of gold is already up $25 an ounce in London, and when the markets open here in New York we're anticipating an even sharper increase. In previous situations like this—for example, the crackdown on Solidarity in Poland back in 1981—the stock market has responded by dropping fast, then recovering slowly over the next month. Already this morning there's talk of U.S. economic sanctions against East Germany. That would hurt companies like Eagle Industries, which have been exporting heavily to that country. Their stock will probably take it on the chin this morning. Happily, we dumped our shares back in April.

Now let's turn to a second hypothetical example: You pick up the morning newspaper and in the middle of page one you see this headline: NEW ENGINE HAILED AS MAJOR BREAKTHROUGH. The story is that a new engine has been developed which can propel a mid-sized car at least fifty miles on just one gallon of unleaded gasoline. The engine was developed by a small company in southern California and unveiled at a press conference the previous afternoon. Accompanying the story is a photograph of the engine itself, flanked on either side by its two inventors; according to the caption, they are engineers who quit their jobs at a major U.S. auto manufacturer, raised a few million dollars to launch the new venture, and after years of struggle are both pleased and stunned to find themselves in imminent danger of prosperity.

Again, most people who read the article do not need more than this information. Here are a few who do, along with the specific intelligence they would receive:

The Chairman of a U.S. Automaker:

The new engine looks to be a great success. Our own people haven't yet finished their analysis, but preliminary results suggest that the engine can be modified for our cars. We are in contact with the inventors to see what sort of licensing arrangement they have in mind. We know for certain that Ford, Chrysler, Nissan, Honda, and Volvo also want licensing agreements; we don't know what terms they want. Our stock has already dropped 6 points on the New York Stock Exchange. Our Wall Street people report that rumors have spread that the inventors are going to sell their rights to the Japanese rather than to us.

The Chief Executive of a Japanese Automaker:

Our people met with the inventors in California at 7 A.M. this morning. The inventors will not sell exclusive rights to the engine—as we predicted they would not—but they are willing to sell us a license to manufacture the engines here in Japan. They have rejected our opening offer of $100 per unit. No doubt they will also be negotiating with our competitors. As you know, we have been aware of this engine for two years, and our engineers have already planned a redesigned vehicle. We can begin production within six months, which should be two to three years before any European auto company and five years before the Americans.

If, in fact, we begin to produce cars equipped with this new engine before our U.S. and European competitors, these countries are likely to retaliate by lowering import quotas on our exports. Thus if we are not careful we could get the engine but lose our markets.

The U.S. Secretary of State:

The new auto engine is two to three times more efficient than current engines. Over time, this could cut U.S. oil imports by $10 billion annually at today's oil prices.

We do not believe that public announcement of the engine will have any impact on your current round of Mideast peace talks. However, if the new engine proves successful over time the Western demand for oil could drop steadily. This, in turn, would send the OPEC economies into a tailspin, leaving some of the key oil-producing countries more vulnerable than ever to radical pressures.

The Managing Director of Briggs-Hanson:

There should be lots of action today when the market opens. Our guys expect that GM and maybe even Chrysler will nosedive, since most people figure they'll find a way to come out last on this. As for the oil companies, they're already down so far that this won't make too much difference, at least in the short run. If this sets off a panic in the Mideast, we could see a fast run-up in the price of gold.

The Oil Minister of Saudi Arabia:

We are in a crisis. This new engine could cut our exports by 20 to 30 percent. The Foreign Minister has called for an emergency OPEC meeting in Vienna tomorrow; he may ask you to represent our country. Our people report widespread sentiment throughout OPEC that we must raise the price of oil now, by at least 30 percent, to offset any future export decline. However, Venezuela and Indonesia are not yet convinced that this is the correct thing to do. Their ambassadors here have already requested meetings with you later this afternoon.

As you well know, thanks to falling oil prices, this year's budget deficit will exceed last year's deficit by at least 25 percent. The construction projects that our kingdom has launched are costing more than we estimated. Thus we may need to delay or even cancel some projects. We believe the U.S. Secretary of State is much concerned that we will choose to target those projects for which U.S. construction companies are the chief contractors. We know that he has told industry leaders he will seek to gain assurance that we will spread delays or cancellations equally.

Now you see the difference between information and intelligence. In each of these examples, the same raw information was enhanced, refined, shaped, and distributed to meet the unique needs of one specific consumer—a consumer being either an individual or an entity—and of no one else. In no two cases was the finished product the same, or could it have been precisely the same. Again, organizing information to meet one consumer's unique needs creates intelligence. And the more effectively and precisely a piece of information is organized to meet the unique needs of its intended recipient, the more complete and successful is the transformation of this information into intelligence.

Whatever delivers information is an information service or system. Likewise, whatever delivers intelligence is an intelligence service or system. And it should be clear from all this that an information service or system is very different from an intelligence service or system. An information system is the sum total of whatever connects an organization or individual to the outside world. It includes the newspapers and magazines that are read, the people one meets with, the telephone calls that are made and received, the observations of key personnel when they travel—literally everything that provides an organization or individual with facts, figures, or "data" of whatever sort from the world outside.

Information systems occur, more or less, naturally. Literally everybody has one. Indeed, an organization or individual cannot help having an information system. Look over someone's shoulder for a week—a housewife's, shopkeeper's, mid-level government bureaucrat's or business executive's, chief executive's, or commander in chief's—and at the end of that time you will be able to draw a diagram of that person's information system. Likewise for an organization. Of course, some individuals and organizations have better information systems than others. Some systems are haphazard; others are carefully, even cunningly constructed. But there is simply no such thing as an individual or organization without an information system.

An intelligence service or system is a less natural, far more complicated structure. To an intelligence outfit, information is merely fuel. It is vital, but not sufficient. Moreover, the fuel has to be the "right" mixture; right, that is, for the particular organization or individual the intelligence outfit is built to serve. Indeed, the intelligence outfit determines just what information the decision-maker will need. The outfit then assures that this information is collected as completely and efficiently as possible, then analyzed and evaluated in light of the organization's or individual's unique needs. Then, finally, comes the make-or-break role for any intelligence outfit: assuring that this organized information—this intelligence—is made available in precisely the right form and at precisely the right time.

Intelligence outfits do not occur naturally. After all, intelligence itself is not a naturally occurring substance like oil. It's a refined product, like gasoline or jet fuel. Any individual, government, or business wanting a steady flow of intelligence must go out and build a service or system from scratch. And if you think of the service or system as though it were a refinery, it's obvious you have to build one that will turn out the products your engines need to run.

Now we can really begin to see why access to intelligence—to organized information—has become so vital to decision-making. Quite simply, by providing a steady flow of organized information an intelligence outfit is uniquely able to help today's policymakers cope with three key features of modern times. Policymakers of earlier times never really had to confront these features, at least not nearly to the same extent.

COPING WITH CHANGE

First, we are living in an age whose dominant force is change itself. Science, technology, economics, politics—these have always been the arenas of change. And today revolutions are taking place in all four arenas. In science, where revolutions usually take place in just one field at a time (such as physics in the early twentieth century), revolutions now are under way in physics, chemistry, mathematics, and biology. In technology, revolutions in microelectronics, communications, materials, and manufacturing processes keep the industrial landscape in a state of constant turmoil. A new product is suddenly obsolete, an industry leader is suddenly on its corporate knees, a little company nobody ever heard of suddenly turns out the state-of-the-art product. Economics itself has been transformed from a dismal science to the acknowledged driving force for national and global change, as government policies for taxation, regulation, currency exchange rates, and public spending power some countries forward and drag others down.

The state of world politics has never been more volatile than it is today. It is scarcely an exaggeration to say that the tectonic plates of global power have broken loose and begun to shift. The U.S.-Soviet relationship has come unglued, the so-called China card seems up for grabs, Western Europe is foundering, and the Pacific Rim is now emerging as a global power center. Come back from lunch and you find another government overthrown somewhere in the world, with the key minister you have courted for years thrown into jail or, literally, blown away, another insurgency started up somewhere else, another hideous attack by terrorists, another rising leader suddenly, astonishingly, on the brink of vast political power.

Result: It has never been more difficult for a government or business to chart and then sustain its course. Simply figuring out what on earth is happening has become a major undertaking. And no sooner do you conclude what the prevailing circumstances are than your conclusions begin to lose their validity. Imagine how hard it would be to choose the best route for a drive from New York to California if the only map you had was so smudged and faded you could scarcely read it. Now imagine that the physical territory of the United States was itself unstable: roads closed and opened with little warning, rivers and mountain ranges shifted overnight, and entire cities rooted up and moved from one location to another. This sounds ridiculous, but in a way this is what our world is like. It is absolutely wild out there. Figuring out what is going on requires a heroic effort, and when you do finally figure it out everything in the world goes ahead and switches around on you. The only thing that you can absolutely, positively count on is change.

COPING WITH THE GLOBAL ARENA

Second, we have reached that point in history when all of us—even the smallest countries and businesses— are operating in the same global arena. The borders are still there, of course. But they no longer provide the safety and protection that they once did. Modern weapons, modern communications, the demand for oil and other raw materials from foreign lands, the scale of modern manufacturing, the sheer size of the world's population—all of these have ended the day when a government or business could stake out its territory and hermetically seal it off to outsiders. It may be a cliché to say that we have become a global village, but it's a cliché that happens to be accurate.

In politics, the titanic struggle between the free world and its enemies—in other words, the Cold War—involves literally every country on earth. There is no place to hide; we are all in this together, on one side or the other, like it or not. Even the so-called neutral nations such as India and Indonesia try to play the superpower rivalry to their advantage. India, for example, manages to get its supercomputers from the United States and its tanks from the Soviet Union. So there is no such thing anymore as a political development in a foreign country that is irrelevant to one's own country; there are only developments that are more or less relevant, and accurately judging the degree of relevance can be a matter of life or death.

The global nature of economic activity has also linked us together, irrevocably, to a degree that has never before existed. A strike, coup, currency shift, or technological breakthrough in one country has an impact far beyond that country's borders. The event needn't be as obvious and as powerful as, say, the U.S. cutting its top personal income tax rate to 28 percent— which has created more wealth in the United States, fueled our demand for imported raw materials and manufactured goods, and thus begun to boost economies throughout the world. The event can be so small and "local" that the foreign impact would be funny if it weren't so devastating to the people affected. When the Coca-Cola Company launched its new-formula Coke onto the U.S. market a couple of years ago, the standard of living in Madagascar very nearly collapsed. Why? Simple: The new Coke contained much less vanilla than the old-formula Coke, and the Madagascan economy rests largely on the production and export of that brown bean; until it changed its formula the Coca-Cola Company was the world's largest buyer of vanilla beans. By turning up their noses at the new Coke, Americans not only forced the Coca-Cola Company to retreat and bring back the old (vanilla-rich) formula, but saved the people of Madagascar from a fast drop in their living standard and, more likely than not, aborted Soviet hopes for destabilizing the suddenly shaky government in Antananarivo.

Because all these global connections now exist—and because they are unavoidable—political and business leaders now must identify and monitor relevant trends and events throughout the world. Truth to tell, there is no such thing anymore as a small country whose interests reach only to its own borders, or perhaps to its immediate and regional neighbors. There are only small countries that are, to a growing degree, at the mercy of incidents and trends all over the globe. A small country whose leaders recognize this can remain a small country; a small country whose leaders fail to recognize this can wind up as an economic basket case or, worse, somebody else's satellite.

Likewise all businesses, regardless of their size, now must view the world as their marketplace. You cannot lay claim to your own patch of territory and expect your competitors to stay out. (Indeed, with the rate of change being what it is you cannot even expect that tomorrow's competitors will be the same as today's.) There is no such thing anymore as, say, a Chicago box manufacturer. There is only a box manufacturer whose corporate headquarters happen to be in Chicago. A company whose chief executive grasps this difference can become a bigger company or, at least, survive. A company whose chief executive fails to grasp this difference is on its way toward being someone else's subsidiary or, worse, going belly-up. As too many chief executives have learned the hard way, in today's environment trouble tends to strike very suddenly; and the downward slope is very steep and slippery.

COPING WITH THE INFORMATION GLUT

The third key feature of modern times is the toughest to grapple with, but in a way the most intriguing of all. We are living in an era of unprecedented access to information. Today's global telecommunications networks move raw information around the world literally at the speed of light. And as the capacity to move information expands, the volume of available information keeps growing to fill this expanding capacity. With more than 10,000 data banks in operation, and with more coming on-line every week, we are reaching the point where the total of human knowledge of nearly every subject or issue now is available to anyone who wants to know it; all you need is a halfway decent computer, a modem, and a telephone line.

In short, raw information from around the world is fairly pouring into government and corporate headquarters, rather like water pouring into the holds of a sinking ship. It comes in by messenger, by telephone and telex, from personnel stationed elsewhere who come in for visits. It comes in through the floor, through the windows, under the desks, over the transoms. It never stops pouring in.

Once in the door, raw information takes on a life of its own. Information has no respect for lines of authority. Any piece of information that reaches any part of any organization moves upward through that organization, like smoke rising through a chimney; block it here and it moves there, always drifting higher and never being fully contained. The result is that today's computer-equipped, senior government and business executives now have—quite literally at their fingertips—raw information that previously would never have reached their organizations in the first place, or would have reached the organization but remained at lower levels, whether it be satellite photographs of enemy troop movements, a shift of key personnel in some competitor's marketing division, or the latest price of this or that commodity halfway around the world.

Today's senior government and business executives are choking on raw information. To their astonishment and growing distress, they are discovering that the only thing as difficult and dangerous as managing a large enterprise with too little information is managing one with too much information.

In this fast-paced, information-driven, global environment, to manage successfully a chief executive needs a mechanism—a management tool, if you will—on which he or she can rely to do four things: First, sort out relevant from irrelevant information. Second, collect and monitor the relevant information as efficiently as possible. Third, process this information for the sole purpose of enhancing that organization's unique decision-making needs. And fourth, assure that the results of this processing—the conclusions, judgments, projections—are made available to the chief executive and other key policymaking executives when they need it and in a form that they can readily absorb. This is what an intelligence outfit is designed to do.

Let's consider each of these steps in turn to see how a government intelligence service or a corporate intelligence system really works.

CHAPTER THREE

HOW INTELLIGENCE WORKS

Good intelligence is power, and so is dynamite. Both are dangerous unless handled wisely.

—Anonymous

No two intelligence outfits are the same. They couldn't possibly be because no two countries or businesses are the same. Nevertheless, the process of intelligence never varies. In all modern outfits this process is composed of four basic steps:

— selecting what needs to be known
— collecting the information
— transforming this collected information into finished products
— distributing these products to policymakers.

These are the steps required to produce modern intelligence no matter what the enterprise or what the issue at hand. There is just no other way to do it. Moreover, the intelligence outfit must complete all four steps, in the correct order, to succeed. If your intelligence outfit misses or trips on any one of these steps, then it takes—and you take—a bad tumble.

SELECTING WHAT NEEDS TO BE KNOWN

One difference between failure and success is not how much you know, but rather how much you know about the right things. And figuring out the right things to know about—which is to say the things that will directly help you to reach a particular objective—is one of the trickiest, least understood, most underrated jobs in the world. What's required to do this job is not so much an expertise in one or another specific subject or issue, but rather the ability to recognize what factors will influence that specific subject or issue. This by itself is a skill—a special kind of expertise. Anyone who knows how to determine what needs to be known to reach one objective can also determine what needs to be known to reach any other objective.

Intelligence professionals have this special expertise. Indeed, intelligence professionals without this expertise aren't professionals. Such professionals always begin with the objectives outlined by the policymakers they serve. Okay, they say to themselves, so we know where the boss wants this enterprise of ours to go. What, then, does he need from us?

Inevitably, some of the things that the chief executive and his lieutenants will need to know will be obvious. For example, let's say the President of the United States makes clear that his objective is to strengthen the free world's ability to defend against a Soviet military attack on Western Europe. Obviously, his intelligence service would need to assess the Warsaw Pact's military capability versus NATO's ability to defeat such an attack. Less obviously, the President's intelligence service would need to assess China's military capability and also reach a judgment on how the Chinese would react in the event of a Soviet attack on Western Europe.

Or, to use a business example, let's say the chief executive of a U.S.-based aluminum manufacturer wants to boost sales of his company's pop-top beverage cans. His intelligence system would need to assess the prospects for growth of the beverage industry. Less obvious is that system's need to assess the prospects that Third-World aluminum producers will move into the canning business; such a move would spell trouble for the U.S. manufacturer, since production costs are generally much lower in the Third World.

This kind of thinking leads rather quickly to a second set of considerations. And it is within this second set that intelligence makes an especially useful contribution. Let's go back to our two original examples. An assessment of NATO's strength would be necessary to achieve the President's objective of enhancing the free world's ability to defend itself against a Soviet military attack. But what factors will influence NATO's strength? One key factor is public support among Europeans for the NATO alliance itself and for the enormous military expenditures required by NATO members to sustain the alliance's strength. And this support is, to a large extent, dependent on the European unemployment rate. Why? Because as the unemployment rate rises, public expenditures for worker benefits also increase, which means that less money is available for defense.

As for our U.S.-based aluminum company's hopes of selling more pop-top cans to the beverage industry, this chief executive's intelligence system had better be assessing developments in the fast-moving composite materials industry. The company's future competitors may not be Third-World aluminum producers at all, but manufacturers of composite materials that will entirely replace aluminum for beverage cans, and in one shot wipe out the aluminum-canning industries in both the United States and the Third World.

This ability to think about subjects and issues in a multidimensional way enables an intelligence outfit to answer the key question: What do our policymakers need to know to achieve their stated objective? Again, it doesn't require expertise in one or another subject or issue so much as it requires expertise in identifying those factors that will affect a given subject or issue. This is a complex, difficult, contentious, energy-consuming sort of process. It cannot be done effectively by policymakers. It isn't that policymakers aren't smart enough; of course they are. It is simply that they haven't got the time.

COLLECTING THE INFORMATION

Once an intelligence outfit has selected what it needs to know, it can get cracking to collect the necessary information. And no matter what the country or the corporation, no matter what the issue, the necessary information falls into three separate and distinct categories.

First, there is **public information**, easily and openly available to anyone who wants it. This includes the sort of statistics and general background material you can get at the public library, from U.S. government agencies such as the State, Commerce, and Treasury departments, from international organizations like the World Bank and the European Community in Brussels, or in respected publications like *The Harvard Business Review*, *The Wall Street Journal*, *The Financial Times*, *Business Week, Fortune,* and *The Economist.* There is a wealth of useful and accurate information available from public sources like these, and you would be amazed at how heavily a good intelligence outfit relies upon them. A good intelligence outfit should rely upon public sources for much of its information. Why spend time and money to manufacture information yourself when it is already waiting and available—and, more often than not, for free—on the shelf?

Second, there is **private information**. This is information not publicly known but legally available to whoever wants it badly enough to seek it out and pull it together. This includes the kind of information and analyses that you can get from talking to knowledgeable people. Let's say an intelligence outfit needs to know what France's economic growth rate is likely to be next year. It need only send one of its officers to talk with that country's best economists; to let him or her meet with those economists in their Paris offices, or buy them lunch at some Left Bank bistro, or subscribe to their expensive but excellent monthly newsletter.

Let's say a country's intelligence service needs to know whether the next attempted coup d'état in Thailand will, unlike its comic opera predecessors, actually bring down the government. Its officers should go to Bangkok and have a quiet session or two with that country's most perceptive politicians. And while there, if they are any good, they will walk their feet off. They will stroll through good and bad neighborhoods, visit markets, read newspapers, wander around the local universities, and so forth to get a sense of the population's mood, its economic conditions, its sense of discontent or tranquility.

Or, if a company in the electronic products business needs to know whether Singapore or Taiwan would be the better choice for its new Asian manufacturing headquarters, its intelligence officers will scrounge around Washington, New York, London, Zurich, and Tokyo, seeking out consultants in these political and financial capitals who have the best grasp of Singapore's and

Taiwan's economic and political prospects. They will check out the world's leading universities to see who among their faculties is worth talking to about the subject. And they will not take the experts' word for it, regardless of their credibility and personal reputations. If the intelligence officers are any good, they will visit the countries themselves, meeting with as many people there from as many walks of life as their time and access permit. They will find out for themselves what is going on, and, more importantly, what is likely to go on in these countries in the months and years to come.

Getting this kind of information takes less genius than effort. It takes a telephone, an airline travel guide, a credit card, and a pair of comfortable shoes. And most of all, it takes a bunch of people each of whom has one of the major qualities of a good intelligence officer: the willingness to move his or her butt and go to wherever the necessary raw information is waiting, almost begging, to be had.

Now the part for which you spy fans have been waiting so patiently. The third and final category is **secret information**—information closely held by those who possess it and not legally available regardless of how much money and effort may be expended to get it. For this stuff, you need spies. Real ones. Let's be clear about one thing right now: Business has no business messing around with spies, secret information, or espionage in any form whatever. It is illegal, immoral, wrong, stupid, and most of all it's just not necessary. The information a business requires to compete successfully in a complex multinational environment is not secret; it is available from the first two categories. Any business executive who thinks he needs secret information to achieve his objectives needs to think again; he is trying to substitute a quick fix for brains and analytic effort.

Governments have different needs. Protecting the national security is a special requirement, and to do so it is sometimes necessary to get one's hands on secrets—not as often as most people think, and not always the kinds of secrets most people imagine—but often enough. Simply put, an espionage unit is the section of a country's intelligence service that is responsible for collecting necessary raw information that is not openly available. Technically, there are two ways to collect secret information—with people and with machinery. Secret information collected by people is called HUMINT, for human intelligence. Secret information collected by people using sophisticated machinery, such as satellites or electronic eavesdropping devices, is called PHOTINT, for photographic intelligence, or SIGINT, for signals or electronic intelligence. In today's world, any major power needs a combination of HUMINT, PHOTINT, and SIGINT to get the sum of necessary secret information.

Even within this unique category of secret information, the driving question remains the same: What do we need to know to achieve the policymakers' objectives? Alas, all too often this key question gets shoved aside in the endless squabble over limited resources—in other words, over who gets the money. During the last few years in Washington, ferocious debates have erupted between those who favor spending more money for HUMINT versus those who want a bigger PHOTINT/SIGINT program. These debates are sterile because they never start off by asking that key question. As we have seen before, when you know what you need to know, you know what you need to collect. And when you know what you need to collect, figuring out which technical means of collection will be most efficient and effective—HUMINT, PHOTINT/SIGINT, or, for that matter, open analysis—is a straight professional judgment call; the debate, as it were, resolves itself.

Secrets are never an end in themselves. This is the key point so many of those who kibitz the intelligence business (and quite a few who have some responsibility for management or oversight) fail to grasp. Secrets are merely one form of raw information, and if you cannot figure out what to do with a particular secret that you are staring at, your intelligence service probably shouldn't have bothered to collect it in the first place.

The problem, of course, is that secrets are addictive. Like peanuts in a bowl, it's hard to eat just one. You can easily wind up stuffing yourself on them and being too full to eat a well-balanced dinner. Likewise, intelligence professionals can become so addicted to secret information that they focus exclusively on this category of raw information; as a result they haven't got the energy or time to collect and analyze open information. And it isn't just the intelligence professionals who are so susceptible to secrets. Consumers of intelligence have been known to become so addicted to secret information that eventually they have lost interest in open information—to the point where they ignored it when it landed on their desks or otherwise hit them between the eyes.

An addiction to secrets, either by a national intelligence service or a country's national-security policymakers, is an indication of looming catastrophe. Too much of what needs to be known to achieve a national objective—any national objective, for any nation—is openly available; to ignore it is to sacrifice depth for titillation. Moreover—and this applies to companies as well as to countries—secrets aren't nearly as secure as they used to be. Organizations have grown so large that even the most closely held secrets are known to scores of people including clerks, secretaries, and aides as well as the policymakers they serve. With so many people in the know—and with so many people in adversary organizations and in the media who want to know—the only question is not whether a secret will leak but when. As for secret new technologies, the rate of change is so high that whatever is secret today is commonplace tomorrow, and soon thereafter obsolete. Simply put, then, the "half-life" of a secret is getting shorter all the time. So to rely on secrets for advantage is to court disaster.

TRANSFORMING COLLECTED INFORMATION INTO FINISHED PRODUCTS

The point of collecting raw information, openly or secretly, is to be able to figure out what it means. And this key step requires the transformation of raw information into finished analytic products—reports that include not only the information itself but also the best available judgments, conclusions, and projections based on this information. Within any intelligence outfit, the analysts are responsible for making this transformation.

Transforming raw information into finished intelligence is itself a step-by-step process. You study the raw material, argue and debate what the material means with your intelligence colleagues, check and recheck the facts, resolve the inevitable inconsistencies in the data, question your original assumptions, assure that as many acknowledged experts as possible have been consulted, develop some tentative theses, and then test these theses time and again until you are confident that the theses are valid.

As you can imagine, all this is a tedious, time-consuming, frustrating, highly contentious business. Even when you manage to get general agreement that a particular "fact" is true—and you don't get such agreement all the time—rarely do the experts agree with one another over what it means. The rule of thumb in intelligence is that to predict the number of interpretations you will hear for an agreed-to fact, just count the number of experts you've consulted and divide—by one. And, of course, within the intelligence outfit itself there is usually a range of opinions among officers. This is very healthy, but also a ferocious pain in the neck for everyone.

An intelligence outfit earns its pay by choosing well—by deciding which experts to back or even whether to ignore them all; by resolving its own internal differences; and by sending forward to policymakers a series of judgments, conclusions, and projections that will, in the end, prove valid. How the differences are resolved, and how the choices are made, marks the difference between a good intelligence outfit and a poor one. After all, there is no question so contentious or controversial that you cannot reach an agreement about it by simply dropping down to the lowest common denominator. For example, if the question is what Europe's economic growth rate will be in the coming year, and half the experts say "higher" while the other half say "lower," you can always get them to agree that in the coming year Europe's economic growth rate will "change." Big deal; that judgment may be accurate, but it is useless to policymakers.

The trick for an intelligence outfit is to resolve differences in a way that is useful to the policymakers. Very often the best way that an intelligence outfit can do this—not merely to protect itself but to help policymakers make the best decisions—is to build differences of opinion into the finished products. The intelligence officers should outline their own judgments; that's what they are being paid for. But they should also tell their policymakers that on this particular issue, expert opinion is divided. They should outline what the differences are, and then explain whether these differences are based on a dispute over the raw facts themselves or over the meaning of agreed-upon facts. Good intelligence officers should never be afraid to include dissenting judgments along with their own. Indeed, it is a disservice to policymakers not to let them know that on the question at hand a range of opinions exists. And when there is general agreement on a particular question or issue—it happens from time to time—it is important for policymakers to know this, too. (Policymakers take note: In these rare instances, watch out. When all the experts agree about something, they are almost always wrong.)

The last step in transforming information into finished intelligence is the actual production of the report itself. When the battles are over and the intellectual bloodstains mopped up, the results must be written out clearly and concisely. No matter how complex or contentious the issue, the report *must* be written so that the policymakers can grasp its essential points easily and quickly, without struggling for hours or doing mental contortions. This is a writing job pure and simple. Obviously, not all good intelligence officers are good writers. So the best intelligence outfits make sure to have at least one or two good writers on board to lend a hand. These writers aren't a frill; they are vital to the production of good intelligence reports, because a report is not effective unless its essence can be grasped easily and quickly by a smart but overworked policymaker.

DISTRIBUTING PRODUCTS TO POLICYMAKERS

There is one word to describe an intelligence outfit that has identified what policymakers need to know, collected all the raw information accurately and efficiently, done a careful and thorough job of analysis and evaluation, and in due course reached sensible, accurate, even brilliant conclusions, judgments, and projections. The word is: useless. The thing that matters—the only thing that matters—is what gets out the door and over to the policymakers. The point of intelligence is to help policymakers guide their organizations to achieve their stated objectives, and if the conclusions of an intelligence outfit do not reach policymakers, those products are of no use whatever. To a chief executive whose country or company is collapsing around his ears, it is of little comfort to know that his intelligence officers are well informed.

We are talking here about the art of marketing and distribution. An intelligence product is no different from any other product. It is the producer's job not only to manufacture but also to market and distribute—to find some way to get that product to its intended consumer. As any manufacturer knows, the world most certainly does not beat a path to your door when you invent a better mousetrap; the world just sits there, waiting for you to reach it. Even then the struggle is not over. As any fledgling sales executive learns, it takes a heroic effort to get someone even to consider a new product, even when it is obviously, visibly, provably in their own best interests to take it. But if you really do have the right product at the right price—and if you hang in there and never give up—then sooner or later they will buy it.

Marketing intelligence to policymakers takes a combination of doggedness, ingenuity, humility, and—on occasion—monumental gall. Policymakers tend to be too busy to devote much time to absorbing finished intelligence; their intentions are good but their time is limited. The urgent pushes aside the important; the piece of data they need right now is what commands their attention, not the careful analysis that will affect events tomorrow. Sometimes—quite often, actually—policymakers must be forced to absorb intelligence that is good for them.

Moreover, different people absorb intelligence in different ways. Some people like to read; others like to be talked to face-to-face. Others prefer listening to audiotapes. Some like charts and assorted "visuals," while others cannot stand them. Videotapes are a big hit with some policymakers, a flop with others. No one form of packaging is better or worse than any other; it is a question of style, taste, even habit.

It is the intelligence officers' job to figure out what will work best for the policymakers they serve, and to orient themselves to whatever turns out to be the answer. The intelligence outfit must adapt itself to the policymakers, not the other way around. An intelligence outfit must be prepared to deliver its products in the form of reports, or audiotapes, or videotapes, or briefings, or charts, or any combination of these. Its officers must be willing and able to catch policymakers wherever they can—at their desks, at breakfast or lunch, at the water cooler, or in the washroom, at their homes, on their way to work, or even on an overseas flight when the policymaker won't be interrupted by telephone calls and has the time and inclination to chat. Intelligence officers must be prepared to do whatever works.

Sometimes nothing works—and this is when intelligence officers really earn their pay. When policymakers are too busy, too distracted, or too far down a primrose path to listen, it is up to their intelligence officers to make them. This is not a job for the fastidious or the fainthearted. This is when an intelligence officer must crash through your gatekeepers, tie you to your chair, and make you listen for your own good and the good of the enterprise. If you haven't got intelligence officers with guts enough to do this when it's necessary, get yourself a new bunch of intelligence officers. You want people who respect, admire, and genuinely like you. You don't want people who are afraid of you or any of your flunky lieutenants. When push comes to shove, your intelligence officers must have the courage and sheer bureaucratic power to get through to you when you need them.

Think of intelligence as a process, rather like manufacturing. It is composed of a series of steps, each one of which must be completed successfully before the next one can be taken. Each step is different, but they all have one thing in common: None of them just happens by itself. You will never just happen to have a new hit product moving by itself onto your company's delivery trucks. Someone will have had to make a series of decisions about the new product, and then managed the entire manufacturing process from the acquisition of raw materials to the design of an eye-catching label.

Likewise with intelligence. You will never just happen to have a vital, finished intelligence product landing all by itself on your desk. Someone will have had to manage the process step-by-step, from selecting what it is that you need to know, to collecting the information, to processing the data, to moving the finished product out their door and onto your desk at precisely the right time and in a format that you can absorb. This is the process of intelligence. This is how intelligence works.

Now let's go inside these outfits to get a better sense of their structure: how they look, feel, and fit within the organizations they serve.

CHAPTER FOUR

WHAT INTELLIGENCE OUTFITS LOOK LIKE

An essential point is not to keep back any intelligence of great consequence . . . but to communicate it without delay to the chief of staff or other officer concerned. The earliest possible information is what is wanted; not only therefore has the news to be got, but the means for transmitting it must be well organized and swift.

—Colonel George Armand Furse,
Information in War: Its Acquisition and Transmission (London, 1895)

SOME wise owl once advised that when you find a restaurant you really like, make it a point never to look at its kitchen. Likewise with intelligence outfits. Indeed, taking an enthusiastic outsider on a tour through the headquarters of an intelligence outfit is an experience that inevitably leaves both parties wishing they had skipped the whole thing:

"Well, what do you think of our little operation?"
"Look, if you don't want to show it to me, just say so."
"What are you talking about? I just did show it to you. This is it."
"Let's not play games. If you're not going to let me see the good stuff, just say so and don't waste my time."
"Really, this is the good stuff. This is where we run it from."
"Let's just drop the matter, okay?"
"Yes, sir."

Get set for a huge disappointment. Physically these outfits don't look all that impressive. In fact, the headquarters of an intelligence outfit is about the most boring-looking place in the world. It's a bunch of offices. More often than not, the offices are older, smaller, more crowded, less elegant, and notably shabbier than the offices of its government's or company's top policymakers. Partly, this is because intelligence outfits have been growing rapidly, and in all rapidly growing organizations space is at a premium. Moreover, since outsiders rarely enter intelligence headquarters, the sorts of imposing offices that are designed to impress them simply aren't necessary; one saves that sort of thing for the State Department or the marketing division. And, finally, intelligence officers tend to have different priorities than their policymaking counterparts. When intelligence officers do have an extra dollar to spend—which is rare—they are more inclined to buy a piece of information with it than a piece of furniture.

At first glance it is hard to believe that anything useful is actually getting done. Half the offices are empty. The other half are occupied by people whose activities are not, shall we say, visually inspiring. Some are hunched over their desks or word processors, often writhing and twisting in their chairs, apparently in some form of agony. Others are tilted back in their chairs, quite tranquil, reading books or magazines whose relevance to the organization's objectives is not immediately obvious. Still others are just sitting there, staring blindly out the window or at a wall. In a few offices you will find groups of people sitting around and talking, sometimes for hours at a stretch. And if you hang around an intelligence headquarters long enough—oh, say, about ten minutes—you will probably see a violent argument erupt in one of the offices or in the corridor.

Don't be fooled by appearances. Half the offices are empty at any given moment because half the employees are out of the building—out of town or, better yet, out of the country—collecting the raw information that will be vital to the success of the enterprise. Those people who are in their offices—writing or reading or staring out the windows and at the walls—are thinking so hard it almost hurts. They may be trying to determine what their policymakers need to know, or how to collect that information. They may already have collected the information and be struggling to figure out what it means— what its impact will be on their own enterprise and on the competition. And those office conversations and water cooler arguments are more than idle chatter. They are the means of exchanging information, trying out ideas and theses, testing conclusions and judgments.

In short, what you are seeing as you walk through the headquarters of an intelligence outfit is a hothouse of focused intellectual creativity. This is what the headquarters of an intelligence outfit is, and this is what such hothouses actually look like. (Okay, okay. You still want to know where the spies hang out, with their miniature cameras, their pistols, their wristwatch walkietalkies, their false passports, and their microdots. First, you only find these things in the intelligence services of some governments. Second, espionage is like sex; there isn't nearly as much of it going on as people like to think. And third, this stuff doesn't go on at headquarters; it goes on elsewhere and only the product is delivered to headquarters. You never get to see the spooks and their equipment when you tour the headquarters of a government's intelligence service because they aren't there.)

Nevertheless, despite their similarities of appearance no two intelligence outfits are the same. Again, no two outfits could be the same because each is built to serve a particular enterprise. And each enterprise has its own unique intelligence needs.

INTELLIGENCE TO SUIT YOUR NEEDS

For example, the United States intelligence service monitors the Soviet Union more closely and completely than does the intelligence service of any other country.

We lead the free world, after all, and the Soviets pose the most direct threat to our own and our allies' security. So we have no choice but to spend an enormous amount of money and effort watching Soviet military forces; if these forces ever start moving in our direction, we absolutely need to know it long before they reach the West German border. And, of course, we need to track such things as the development of Soviet weapons, the sale of these weapons to Third-World countries, Soviet diplomatic initiatives, and a range of internal Soviet trends including economic growth rates, incidents of civil unrest, and the availability of food and oil. We do all this to enable our policymakers to chart a course that will achieve their number-one security objective: deterring Soviet military aggression against ourselves and our allies.

But at the same time, as the world's leading economic and technological power we compete directly with our free-world allies for access to raw materials and to markets for our manufactured products. So our intelligence service needs to monitor a wide range of non-Soviet issues including the political stability of the suppliers of our raw materials, the trade policies of our key industrial competitors, the economies of the major overseas customers for U.S. products, the impact of foreign technological breakthroughs on our own interests, and scientific trends that over time may have important commercial as well as military applications. In short, as a superpower we have intelligence needs that require a big, broadly based service to fulfill.

In contrast, a small country with narrower interests has a smaller range of intelligence needs. Israel, for example, puts the bulk of its intelligence effort into monitoring the military strength of its belligerent Arab neighbors. What efforts the Israelis make to track Soviet developments focus largely—and quite logically—on Soviet political initiatives in the Mideast itself and on the Soviet Union's Jewish emigration policies.

And to take a completely opposite political example, the Soviet Union itself puts the bulk of its national intelligence effort into spying on its own citizens. To be sure, the KGB is one big, globally oriented monster of an operation. It has agents in every country—not only the traditional type of spooks, but more and more yuppie types with a grasp of high technology and access to good tailors so they don't stick out at conferences and cocktail parties—and these agents gather information on a wide range of issues. But the main thrust of the KGB's effort is internal. It always has been, and probably it always will be.

In business, the closest things to the superpowers in terms of intelligence requirements are the Japanese trading companies, or *sogo shosha*. Mitsubishi, Mitsui, Sumitomo, Nissho-Iwai, and the others understand intelligence-as-organized-information, take it seriously, and pour an awful lot of money and manpower into collecting, analyzing, and distributing intelligence to key executives. Indeed, the effective use of business intelligence by the trading companies is one key reason Japanese industry has done so well during the past couple of decades. More precisely, from their headquarters in Tokyo, each of these *sogo shosha* monitors the prices of key raw materials, from oil to copper to corn. They monitor the activities of their competitors for these materials, as well as political developments in the producing countries.

Indeed, they monitor everything that could possibly affect their company's, and their country's, access to the raw materials Japan must have to fuel its economic engine. At the same time, on behalf of their manufacturing partners, the trading companies monitor economic trends and technological developments in foreign countries and companies that manufacture competing products, from turbines to tennis rackets to computers.

The big, privately held grain-trading companies also have global intelligence requirements. Continental and Cargill in the United States, André in Switzerland, Louis Dreyfus in France, and Bunge in Argentina monitor worldwide weather patterns, crop conditions, harvest schedules, storage levels, shipping rates, government subsidy programs, and all the other global supply-and-demand factors that key grain executives need to know so they can move, swiftly and silently, when opportunity comes calling. Indeed, in the fast-paced and uniquely secretive world of grain trading, these guys need to move when opportunity first pokes its head over the horizon.

Manufacturing companies have the most sharply focused intelligence requirements because, whatever their size, they are by definition turning out specific and unique products (as opposed to fungible commodities) for sale in specific markets. Whether it is electronics, pharmaceuticals, or automobiles, a manufacturing company needs to monitor what its competitors are doing and might be planning to do, where the new competition could come from, what their customers are doing and saying about their product, political and economic developments in current markets, trends that could close these markets or open new ones, what the company's various suppliers are up to, and selected technological and scientific projects whose outcome could create new problems—or opportunities—for the manufacturing company.

NO TWO STRUCTURES ARE THE SAME

The actual structure of government and corporate intelligence outfits reflects their focus. For example, the U.S. Intelligence Community has an analytic coordinating unit at its topmost level called the National Intelligence Council. This small council is made up of about fifteen National Intelligence Officers, each of whom holds one of the portfolios that reflect the entire Community's focus. So, we have National Intelligence Officers for every geographic region of the world: the Soviet Union, Europe, Latin America, Africa, the Mideast, Asia. And we have National Intelligence Officers for key subjects that cut across geographic lines such as economics, counterterrorism, conventional military forces, and strategic (nuclear) forces. Through these officers, the National Intelligence Council helps to select those areas and issues that need to be monitored within each portfolio, then selects data from the various U.S. intelligence collection agencies—which include the Central Intelligence Agency, the National Security Agency, the Defense Intelligence Agency, the individual military service intelligence units, and a few others we mustn't talk about. Then the council plays the role of honest broker. That is, the council sorts through the various differences of judgment and opinion, works out its main theses, accommodates dissenting views, and ultimately prepares for the President and his top national security advisers the so-called National Intelligence Estimates, which reflect the entire community's conclusions, judgments, and projections about key countries, subjects, and issues.

Other parts of the U.S. Intelligence Community are unique to government. For that small but vital portion of information we need about our adversaries that is not openly available, we rely on our elite corps of intelligence operations officers. These are the dedicated, highly trained men and women who are stationed overseas, under "cover" and often at considerable risk to themselves and their families, and who provide the role models for authors of spy novels. In addition, a counterintelligence staff tries to keep enemy intelligence services from penetrating the organization itself. And, finally, a covert action unit provides policymakers with the ability to respond operationally when the situation calls for more than diplomacy but less than war.

To serve their broad commercial interests, the Japanese trading companies—*the sogo shosha*—have created vast overseas data-collection networks. Indeed, every branch office of every trading company operates like an information vacuum cleaner, sucking in statistics, documents, brochures, articles from technical and current events magazines, reports delivered at industrial and scientific conferences attended by one or another Japanese executive, and even gossip picked up at dinner parties or on the golf course. Some of these trading company operations are substantial; the Mitsubishi intelligence staff in New York takes up two entire floors of a Manhattan skyscraper.

Raw information collected by Japanese executives stationed overseas is transmitted daily—sometimes hourly or even by the minute—back to Japan. There, at company headquarters, a senior intelligence staff collates this raw material and shapes finished intelligence products for key policymakers within the trading company. And, yes, in one form or another—informally as well as formally—much of this intelligence is shared with executives at the trading companies' manufacturing partners and with selected Japanese government officials, who move the information around still more.

The big grain-trading companies have intelligence units whose structures are similar to those of the Japanese trading companies. In essence, each grain-trading company has branch offices throughout the world, and each branch is responsible for collecting and transmitting intelligence from within its territory to company headquarters. Cargill receives about 14,000 messages each day from its 250 branch offices; these are routed to the various trading desks at headquarters in Minneapolis—the wheat desk, the corn desk, and so forth—for collation, synthesis, and use. Moreover, the grain-trading companies have been especially adept at reaching beyond their own staffs for key intelligence. They contract with topflight professional weather services to monitor and predict rainfall levels in key crop-producing countries. They buy crop forecast reports from competing services, then compare these various projections with one another and with their own computer-modeled projections. And they hire private economists and political risk analysts to backstop and supplement their own, highly sophisticated collection and analytic efforts.

Most U.S. manufacturing companies do not have clearly designated, formally structured intelligence outfits. To be sure, this doesn't mean that most U.S. companies do not collect information, process it into intelligence, and then distribute finished products to policymakers. As we pointed out earlier, a company cannot help performing these functions. The marketing division, the sales force, the economics group within the financial division, and the research-and-development unit each collects, processes, and in one form or another organizes and distributes information. After all, something need not be called an intelligence outfit to be one. But the absence of formally structured, centrally coordinated intelligence outfits in most U.S. corporations means these companies cannot do intelligence work very efficiently.

A growing number of U.S. companies now have formal units that focus on "competitor intelligence"—which means knowing what the other guys in the industry are up to. Pfizer, IBM, International Paper, and other forward-looking companies now have organized small units to collect, process, and distribute intelligence about their competitors' plans, products, and financial prospects. These units are positioned, variously, in the marketing division, the planning group, or even in the research and development organization.

A few innovative U.S. companies have set up genuine full-service intelligence units headed by chiefs who report directly to the chief executive. For example, Motorola Corporation has set up a unit that bears a striking resemblance to the U.S. government's National Intelligence Council. This unit has about a half-dozen professionals who, like the national intelligence officers in Washington, hold portfolios that match the profile of the company's key objectives and interests. One officer keeps track of European business developments in areas of particular interest to the company; another does the same for Asia. Yet another officer focuses exclusively on developments in specific fields of technology that the company has singled out for special corporate attention and investment. There is an officer who monitors the trade policies of key countries, including the United States itself. And, in an especially clever move, Motorola's intelligence chief has assigned one officer to debrief the company's own executives each time they return from overseas or even domestic trips. This assures that all the little tidbits, all those scribbled notes, brochures, articles, reports, and so forth that traveling business executives come home with are collected, evaluated, distilled, and checked against one another. Result: Important new information is retained rather than lost, while new trends are discerned at the earliest possible moment. This is business intelligence at its best.

In both government and business, the intelligence service or system is the purest, most visible reflection of that organization's perceived interests. Look at the service or system—its focus, what its people are working at, what is being monitored, what kinds of reports are being written and to which policymakers these reports are distributed—and you have a remarkably accurate picture of the environment in which that organization perceives itself to be operating. Why does the U.S. government have a world-wide focus that is centered on the Soviet Union? Because our leaders perceive that the Soviet Union is the greatest threat to our security. And why does the Soviet Union's ruling Communist Party focus so much of the KGB's efforts internally? Because the Party's leaders know that there is no serious threat to their country or to their own security from the United States or from any other free-world country. The chief threat comes, as it does in any dictatorship, from the Soviet Union's own oppressed citizens. And the Japanese trading companies send so many of their intelligence-collecting executives to the United States because the chief executives of these *sogo shosha* accurately perceive that this country is and will remain Japan's biggest market and chief manufacturing competitor.

To be sure, if the organization has a perception of its interests and its adversaries that is flawed, the intelligence outfit will be focused on the wrong things. The outfit will be focused on the wrong things even if the policymakers' perception of their organization's environment is valid, but the policymakers have not communicated this perception to their intelligence outfit. In either instance, you have found yourself an organization with one huge problem on its hands.

One final note on the structure of intelligence outfits. They are never stable. An organization's focus is forever shifting, and the intelligence outfit—more than any other unit of the organization—must shift in response. For example, ten years ago most government intelligence services did not have special units that focused exclusively on counterterrorism; they didn't need such units. Now counterterrorism units are a standard feature of Western intelligence services, and rightly so. Ten years from now perhaps we won't need such units. Perhaps we will need to focus instead on the threat from genetically engineered biological weapons systems. Within the corporate world, a company may now be focusing on, say, the use of gallium arsenide for computer chips; it may have someone who does nothing but track developments in the gallium arsenide field. Five years from now these people may be redirected so that the company may track the development of chips made from even more exotic compounds such as germanium arsenide or, perhaps, antimony silicon.

Intelligence outfits are always setting up new units,

taking apart older ones, retraining people who are experts in subjects that are no longer crucial, bringing in new experts when the old ones cannot be retrained fast or well enough. It's a joke among intelligence officers that when you leave town on business, the office is going to look different when you return. Actually, it's not so funny. Let's just say that the more experienced intelligence officers make it their business to keep close tabs on headquarters developments while they are traveling.

There is one other feature common to the headquarters of intelligence services and systems: an atmosphere of heavy, creepy, almost frightening tension. You can feel and even smell it, just as you can feel and smell the tension when you walk into a house whose occupants are having an especially bitter marital dispute. In an intelligence headquarters this atmosphere never changes. Day after day, week after week, the air seems electrically charged, fairly crackling with tension. To be sure, intelligence officers are as cheerful and good-humored a bunch of people as you will meet anywhere. They laugh easily and crack jokes as well as anyone. And the tension isn't there because intelligence officers see dangers to their organization more clearly, or sooner, than policymakers—although this is sometimes the case. Nor is the atmosphere tense because intelligence officers are especially high-strung people, although this, too, is sometimes the case.

The root cause of this unrelenting tension lies in the relationship between intelligence and policymaking. It is a unique and inherently tense relationship. The key to managing an intelligence outfit successfully—to assuring that it gives you, the policymaker, the organized information you need to lead your enterprise toward the objectives you have chosen to reach—lies in understanding why this tension is there. So let's take a closer look at what it's like to lead an organization that has its own intelligence outfit.

CHAPTER FIVE

INTELLIGENCE AND POLICYMAKING

"There's just one thing I think you ought to know before you take on the job. And don't forget it. If you do well you'll get no thanks and if you get into trouble you'll get no help. Does that suit you?"

"Perfectly."

"Then I'll wish you good-afternoon."

W. SOMERSET MAUGHAM,
Ashenden: The British Agent

BUILDING an intelligence outfit into your organization is like having a new baby in the family. Over time the rewards are incalculably huge and in your heart of hearts you know this. But at least once a day you are sure you have made a terrible mistake and that the strain will do you in; you cannot imagine how you ever let yourself get into this mess, and if there was a decent way out you would take it. Then, just when you have absolutely had it, something wonderful happens—the baby smiles, or someone says the baby's cute and looks like you—and you come to your senses, settle down, and realize you have done the right thing. You even find yourself thinking of doing it again.

For a combination of reasons, of all the management tools available to chief executives and their policymaking lieutenants an intelligence outfit is the trickiest, most frustrating, hardest-to-handle of them all. The rewards of having an intelligence outfit are inestimable, but on a day-to-day basis the strain is a killer. Let's look at the reasons it is so hard to lead an organization that has its own intelligence outfit, and consider what you can do to ease the burden and even enhance your chances of success.

YOU'VE GOT TO KNOW WHERE YOU'RE GOING

We said earlier that a modern intelligence outfit is like an on-board navigation system. And we pointed out that an on-board navigation system cannot guide a ship or airplane from one point on earth to another until the captain and his crew have accurately punched in the course coordinates of their chosen destination. If the captain and his crew don't know where they want to go, even the world's finest navigation system is useless.

Likewise with any government or business. If the policymakers don't know where they want to go, even the world's finest intelligence outfit cannot help. It is the policymakers' responsibility to know where they want the organization to go—to decide what the organization's objectives should be. If policymakers do not know where they want to take their organizations they shouldn't have their jobs in the first place. Moreover, policymakers are responsible for articulating the objectives they have set for their organization. Sometimes it makes sense to keep these objectives a secret from your competitors. It never makes sense to keep these objectives a secret from your intelligence officers.

The more clearly, precisely, and completely you articulate the objectives you have set, the better able your intelligence outfit will be to do its job. So, for example, if you are the chairman of a big U.S. bank and your objective is to write off within the next six months 30 percent of the total debts you are owed by Third-World countries—say so. Then your intelligence outfit can focus on assessing which of these debtor countries is likely to make at least some token payments during the coming months and which won't cough up a nickel for years to come. With this assessment in hand, you are in a strong position to decide which 30 percent of outstanding Third-World debts to write off and which 70 percent to roll over.

Or, if you are the leader of a Third-World country that is up to its eyes in debt to various U.S. and European banks, and your objective is to get at least some of these banks to write off the debt—make this clear to your intelligence outfit. Then the outfit can try to assess the current policies of each creditor bank to tell you which ones are on the verge of decisions and which banks don't plan to take any drastic actions in the coming months. And if you are the President or Prime Minister of a country whose leading banks have mindlessly poured their assets into assorted Third-World countries and you are scared stiff that one of the big debtors will do something really stupid and bring the world economy crashing down—let your intelligence outfit know that this is on your mind. Then the outfit will know to track financial developments especially closely, so that you will be tipped off fast to impending political decisions in Mexico, Peru, Brazil, Zaire, or wherever. If your outfit is any good, and if luck is on your side, you will be tipped off early enough to block the decision, or modify or reverse it, or do whatever you and your policymaking advisers conclude is best.

Setting objectives and articulating them is the essence of leadership. It is also the hardest thing to do. Since an intelligence outfit *must* know your objectives to operate, the intelligence officers are forever on your back. They always want to know your current thoughts. They want to know if the statement you issued yesterday, or the offhand comment you made at this morning's staff meeting, reflects a shift of priorities or even a change of direction. They try to pin you down more often, and more precisely, than you like. They have to do this to do their job. But for you, the policymaker, this can be a ferocious nuisance, even a source of genuine discomfort. It forces you to say out loud—in private, but out loud—things you would rather not say, either because you are afraid the wrong people will find out or because, frankly, you just don't know what your objective should be. If you are not careful you find yourself avoiding your intelligence officers. They will know you are avoiding them, and they will know why.

Still worse, when things go badly—and things always go badly for organizations whose leaders haven't got clear objectives—it is all too easy to blame the intelligence outfit for whatever setbacks or disasters occur. Intelligence outfits make excellent scapegoats; nobody outside the organization really knows what they're doing, and the first ethic of intelligence is to do the best you can, keep your mouth shut, and never go public with your own views of your policymakers and their shortcomings. This is a good and necessary ethic, but its by-product is often a steady, high level of tension.

YOU MUST GRASP THE DIFFERENCE BETWEEN WHAT YOU *WANT* TO KNOW AND WHAT YOU *NEED* TO KNOW

Top-level policymakers always know precisely what they want to know. And, to put this as delicately as possible, they are not shy about asking. Indeed, their questions never stop coming. They come in all day long at intelligence headquarters by telephone, in memos, and at meetings. They come at night, when the officers have put their kids to bed and just settled down for a quiet hour of reading or talking or television-viewing. They come in even later at night, when the officers have locked their doors and gone to bed themselves. When a policymaker decides he wants to know something, he wants to know it yesterday, if not sooner:

"I hope I haven't woken you up, but who's going to win the election in West Germany next Sunday?"

"Sorry about pulling you out of your meeting, good buddy, but who's going to be the next foreign minister down in Australia?"

"What's the price of gold going to be in three weeks? How about giving me an answer before lunch, please."

"When do your people figure the Japanese will make that breakthrough in ceramic engines? What are we paying you guys for, anyway?"

You cannot blame a policymaker for wanting to know these things. Unfortunately, the answers to questions like these are not obtainable. Nobody knows who is going to win an election in a foreign democracy; for that matter, within one's own country the so-called experts never agree with one another. So how can an intelligence outfit do more than summarize the experts' judgments? As for who the next foreign minister of a country is going to be, the curious policymaker is getting too far in front of events; it's a fair bet he's asking for an answer before the choice has been made. Nobody knows what the price of gold will be three weeks hence. And it is just about impossible to predict when an expected industrial or technological breakthrough is going to come about; the scientists and engineers themselves usually are stunned when it actually happens. Just look at the astounding rate of progress being made right now in the field of superconductors. The scientists themselves can scarcely believe it.

Moreover, even if accurate answers were obtainable to such questions, they wouldn't do the policymaker much good. They would be more interesting than useful. To use the example of upcoming elections in West Germany, what a U.S. policymaker really *needs* to know three weeks prior to election day is not who is going to win—which is not knowable—but rather an analysis of the various forces that will influence whoever emerges victorious in Bonn. What will be the economic environment in which the new leader will operate? How will the Soviets respond to this or that outcome? In short, what will be the range of options available to the new leader regardless of which party he heads? The answers to questions like these enable U.S. policymakers to chart a course.

Likewise with the example of the next Australian foreign minister. The question is not so much his identity as it is Australia's current view of its national role. The new minister will be a reflection of that view, more than a shaper of it. The same with the price of gold in three weeks. What a chief executive really needs to know is what the world economic picture will look like; again, the price of gold will be a reflection of that picture rather than the shaper of it. And finally, since a technological breakthrough cannot be timed to the week or month, what a chief executive needs to know is the level of effort his competitors are devoting to the problem. And he needs an analysis of how the market would respond to such a development, along with the impact on his own company.

The conflict never ends between what you, the policymaker, want to know and what your intelligence officers think you need to know. Again, it is not that policymakers are less subtle or sophisticated than intelligence officers. It is simply the nature of their respective roles. You policymakers are on the front lines all the time. You need to make decisions, often quickly. The urgent shoves aside the important. You have too much to do and too little time in which to do it. From your perspective, the intelligence people are always balking, always making excuses for why they cannot answer a "simple" question, always trying to force you to delve more deeply into a subject than your time or inclination permits. This gap is not a solvable problem but an aggravating, tension-ridden condition you can only learn to live with.

The best approach is to accept that your intelligence outfit exists not to humor you, but to help you reach your objectives. You know best where to go; the intelligence officers know best what information you need to get there. Don't try to divert your intelligence outfit so its officers are searching for answers they judge cannot be found. Indeed, give them leeway to choose the questions. Remember that knowing what questions to ask is an intelligence skill, and part of what you are paying them to do. Moreover, when your intelligence officers feel they have got the leeway to ask the questions they think are right—and you are willing to listen to their answers—you will be surprised at how willing they will be to stretch themselves to find out the things you want, but don't really need, to know.

YOU MUST HAVE THE GUTS TO FACE FACTS

No plan emerges unscathed from its collision with reality. The world is too complicated, too sloppy, too unpredictable. There is always something that doesn't work out the way it was supposed to. And it is the intelligence officers who deliver the bad news to policy-makers. After all, they are the ones who are monitoring relevant trends and developments. Thus they are the first to know when your plan starts to go haywire or even just a bit off course.

Let's say that a candidate is elected President of the United States on the promise of restoring some form of détente with the Soviet Union. He lowers trade barriers, cuts the U.S. defense budget, cools the rhetoric, and stops supporting pro-West insurgents in various Third-World countries. But the Soviets respond by boosting their military budget and funneling more advanced weaponry to their Third-World allies who are trying to crush pro-West forces. Who gets to tell the President how his policy is working? The intelligence officers, of course. Or, if a candidate is elected President on the promise of standing up to the Soviets and reversing his predecessor's policy, who tells him that the pro-West insurgents he has decided to support are, alas, a disorganized bunch of crooks who lack the military discipline to topple a fruit stand? Again, intelligence.

It is the same in business. The chief executive of a U.S. office-equipment manufacturer decides to export his company's personal computers to Europe. Since the PCs are a hot item in the U.S. market, the chief executive personally orders that no changes whatever be made to the machines built for shipment overseas. But after three months it's clear that the Europeans are not buying the computers because their design is, well, un-European. Who gets to tell the boss his great plan is flopping? You guessed it. Or, imagine that you are the chairman of a breakfast-cereal company and you've committed the company to a long-term contract for purchase of some new artificial sweetener. Now there are indications—nothing concrete, just indications—that a rival supplier will soon be able to market a newer artificial sweetener that is every bit as good as the one you're buying, but cheaper. If your cereals-industry competitors move swiftly, their costs may be lower than yours. This is not a good situation at all for your company, and if you have an intelligence outfit, it is this outfit that gets to deliver the bad news to you.

It isn't always the wisdom of a policy or plan that's the problem. Quite often a policy or plan is sensible, well conceived, and competently executed. It is just that things do not always work out precisely the way one expects them to. In a way an intelligence outfit serves as a performance-evaluation mechanism, and no policymaker likes to have his performance evaluated. Tensions run especially high when the plan itself is based on one policymaker's strong personal bias. The policymaker inevitably views any criticism of the plan as a personal attack or, in the political arena, as an attack on his ideology.

For intelligence officers, the trick is to bring policymakers the bad news they need to know without seeming to attack the entire policy. After all, no policymaker takes kindly to criticism or to bad news that seems like criticism. It isn't that policymakers are especially flawed human beings; it's just that they are busy, under immense pressure, and sick to death of being told why things are not going according to plan. If you're not careful, you start to view your intelligence officers as your adversaries—as the people who know too much about whatever is not going well. Soon you don't trust your intelligence officers. And when this trust is broken, so, too, is the intelligence outfit's ability to participate usefully.

Look at it from the intelligence officers' point of view.

Being cut off by policymakers isn't much fun. The telephones stop ringing. Meetings, lunches, and dinner parties take place to which they no longer are invited. They hear themselves being referred to as "them" rather than "our intelligence guys."

So what does an intelligence officer do who finds himself being cut off or left out? Does he trim his sails and not deliver too much bad news? Does he try to sugarcoat his conclusions, judgments, and projections? Or does he ram them down the policymaker's throat, and pray the policymaker will understand that in fact he's trying to help? There are no easy answers to these questions. Again, it is not a situation but rather a condition that intelligence officers live with all the time.

BRACE YOURSELF FOR A STEADY DIET OF DANGER

Like any good on-board navigation system, an intelligence outfit is forever sweeping the horizon and blipping every time it finds something that could, possibly, be on a collision course. And the fact is, there is always something out there. Always. The result is that your intelligence outfit will forever be inundating you with analyses of potential problems. The economies of West Africa are weakening. On some Caribbean island a left-wing politician is gathering huge crowds at his rallies; the Cubans may be shipping in small arms. We've just received a report that a key European leader is not as healthy as he looks. A company in Singapore may start to manufacture a product sort of similar to our product. There may be more natural gas than anybody thinks in

Scandinavia, and the impact on our company's costs will be substantial. Japan is about to shift its trade policy, and our competitors are better positioned than we are to take advantage of it.

An intelligence outfit never stops sweeping the horizon for potential problems. Nor should it. And an outfit never stops passing on its reports—its conclusions, judgments, projections—to policymakers. Nor should a good intelligence outfit ever stop reporting, or even slow down the pace of its reporting. But it doesn't take long before even the most devoted and intelligence-minded policymaker comes down with a bad case of intellectual indigestion. From the policymaker's view, the intelligence guys are finding problems everywhere; they are manufacturing potential problems just so they have something to talk about—to make themselves more important. The policymaker says, Relax! Most of these potential problems won't ever happen. The intelligence officer replies, You may be right, but if you're wrong we're dead; you'd better look at this. The policymaker says, You're driving me nuts. The intelligence officer shoots back, You'll be sorry. Both are right.

As a policymaker, the trick is to keep your intelligence outfit revved up without letting yourself be buried alive in the resulting avalanche of reports, warnings, and alerts. This isn't hard if you go at it with the right attitude. Keep in mind that to an intelligence officer, the absolute worst thing that can happen is a failure to warn of some looming danger. The rule of thumb in intelligence is: When in doubt, warn. It is better to be called a Nervous Nellie than a nincompoop. As a policymaker, the worst mistake you can make is to frighten off your intelligence officers—to make them afraid to come to you with potential dangers. So when they come in to warn you of something you don't think will happen, go easy on them. Hear them out. You may change their minds. Or they may change your mind. Even by discussing the issue, you may gain some new insight. And in dismissing a perceived danger, you just may see an opportunity you otherwise would have missed.

DON'T BE AFRAID OF MAKING "DUMB" DECISIONS

As a policymaker, there are just two things you can do with good intelligence that are guaranteed to earn you the contempt of your intelligence outfit: nothing and something.

An intelligence officer wants to see results; he wants his findings, facts, judgments, and projections to lead to action. When his report lands on your desk, the intelligence officer wants you to stop whatever you are doing, read the report, then reach for your telephone, call together a crisis-command group, and—go. But as a policymaker, you have an entirely different perspective. Your job is to reach established objectives, and to do this you must marshal your own and your organization's energies. You must ruthlessly choose when *not* to act—when to suffer a small defeat or setback in pursuit of the larger gain.

Moreover, much of the intelligence that flows to you will be relevant but not critical. It may focus on an issue of less than decisive impact to the organization, or it may include information on a decisive issue that is new but not vital. So as a good policymaker you will often decline to take immediate action on a particular intelligence report. But to the officer who prepared that report—at great effort and perhaps at great risk—this decision to do nothing will smack of "ignoring" intelligence. It isn't, really. It is just good steady leadership. After all, in any organization you achieve your goals by doing nothing 90 percent of the time. It's the other 10 percent that makes the difference. But the intelligence officer is not being paid to separate the 90 percent from the 10 percent; his job is to provide the intelligence so that you, the policymaker, can decide what to do with it.

Even when you act you will earn the disapproval of your intelligence outfit most of the time because the actions you take will rarely track totally, completely, 100 percent with the intelligence that has been provided to you. That is, the actions you take will differ somewhat from the actions that someone who reads *only* the intelligence report would expect you to take.

After all, managing an enterprise is a sloppy sort of thing to do. You cut corners, make deals, and juggle interest groups. You rarely, if ever, suffer total, unconditional defeat. And even more rarely do you enjoy total, unconditional victory. You always settle for something less than the whole loaf. Nor can you always explain your decisions to everyone's satisfaction, for no one subordinate or division can see the world from your own unique perspective as the leader. Intelligence is no exception to this. When an intelligence outfit sends a report to policymakers, it wants and expects that action will be taken on this report—and on nothing except this report. Yet a policymaker who acts on his intelligence reports—and on nothing else—is a fool. You must mix in your own judgment and experience, and in the end your own gut feeling for what course of action will be in the organization's best interests. Once again, the result is steady tension between intelligence and policymaking.

NEVER, NEVER COOK THE BOOKS

Not all people are honest, and not all honest people are honest all the time. Policymakers and intelligence officers suffer from the same frailties as everybody else. And when they are dishonest—which, alas, from time to time they are—they create a mess.

There are two ways in which a policymaker can be dishonest with intelligence: passively and actively. Passive dishonesty happens when a policymaker willfully ignores an intelligence report because he doesn't like its conclusions, judgments, or projections—because he finds them inconvenient or otherwise troublesome. We are not talking about a policymaker who disagrees with an intelligence report, but rather about a policymaker who knows in his heart that the intelligence is accurate but who refuses to face up to it. Ignoring intelligence is not hard. In fact, it is all too easy. You simply leave the offending report on the bottom of the pile. You don't pass it on to anyone else. You don't do anything at all—except put the safety of your country or your company at risk.

Active dishonesty is worse. This happens when a policymaker directly interferes with the preparation of intelligence. He can do this by pressuring the intelligence outfit to give him specific conclusions and projections that will justify a course of action already taken or decided upon. For example, a U.S. President hell-bent on signing an arms-control treaty with the Soviet Union could order an intelligence report that would focus exclusively on judging how European public opinion would respond to the signing of an arms pact. Since public opinion in Europe responds favorably to the signing of just about any U.S.-Soviet arms pact—no matter what its content or the chances for Soviet compliance with its provisions—such a report would inevitably lend support to the President's policy.

Or a policymaker can order his intelligence outfit *not* to prepare a report on some particular issue, for fear its conclusions, judgments, and projections will upset a course of action already taken or decided upon. To use this same example, a President hell-bent on an arms treaty could order his intelligence outfit not to prepare a report that would offer judgments and projections on the chances for Soviet compliance with provisions of the proposed agreement.

This is a two-way street. Intelligence officers can be just as dishonest as policymakers. The obvious form of dishonesty comes when the officers knowingly and willfully skew their judgments and projections. This can happen when the assembled verified facts invalidate the outfit's own earlier judgments and projections. For example, an intelligence service that has submitted three consecutive annual reports projecting continued political stability in a certain Third-World country may balk at submitting a fourth report that contradicts the previous three, showing new evidence that an insurgency has for years been gaining strength in the countryside and that the rebels now stand on the brink of seizing power. A corporate intelligence outfit whose previous report concluded that a certain country would welcome a major investment—resulting in construction of a multimillion-dollar factory—may hesitate to report new evidence that this country's government is about to nationalize all foreign-owned businesses.

A less obvious form of dishonesty—but an equally dangerous and reprehensible one—comes when the intelligence officers withhold judgments and projections from their policymakers because of their own distaste for what they know or believe those policymakers will do. In theory, intelligence officers are like professional military officers; they are apolitical. In practice, this is often the case—but not always. A "liberal" intelligence officer who senses that his "conservative" policymaker is just itching for an excuse to bash the Soviet Union may not pass on information that confirms reports of Soviet cheating on an arms treaty. Likewise, a "conservative" intelligence officer may withhold from his "liberal" policymaker evidence that the Soviets have taken quiet but meaningful steps to comply not only with the letter but with the spirit of an arms agreement.

It is the same in business. An intelligence officer who personally opposes the new diversification plan that has been proposed may be tempted to withhold evidence that the market for the company's current line of products is evaporating. Or an officer who favors diversification may withhold evidence that a fortune is to be made by sticking with the current product line—that competitors who have diversified are losing their shirts.

All of this is cooking the books. In fact, it happens very rarely. But the danger is so great, and the consequences so horrendous, that the fear of cooked books is ever-present. Policymakers and intelligence officers are permanently, inherently suspicious of one another, and this suspicion itself becomes a major source of tension.

As a policymaker, you must resist all temptation to interfere with intelligence solely to assure that the finished products have the right "spin" to them. It isn't worth it—ever. And you must make clear to your intelligence officers that their job is to call the shots the way they see them, and not to try and second-guess what you want to hear. And if you find out that your intelligence outfit has put a "spin" on some report to suit the personal preferences of one or another officer, find out who let this happen and fire him.

DON'T HOG THE CREDIT

Every so often—even in the goofiest, most screwed-up countries and corporations—the system works perfectly. The intelligence outfit is miles ahead of everyone else. A problem is identified, monitored, analyzed, and evaluated. A report is prepared that is brief, pungent, packed with facts, and laden with judgments and projections that not only cry out for action, but point the way toward a series of effective steps that even the most dim-witted policymaker can grasp and follow. And the policymaker performs brilliantly. He absorbs the intelligence, gathers together a team, formulates a plan of action even the intelligence officers applaud, executes that plan flawlessly, and wins if not a whole loaf, then just about. Result: increased tension between intelligence and policymaking. It never fails.

For example, an intelligence service discovers a plot to blow up one of their country's overseas installations. It tells the policymakers, who shake their heads and ask, Where? So the intelligence officers tell the policymakers which country, and they ask, When? The intelligence officers tell the policymakers when and they ask, How? The intelligence officers tell them with a bomb concealed inside a truck, and the policymakers ask, What kind of truck? A green Mercedes-Benz, the intelligence officers report, and the policymakers ask, What license plate? So they are told the plate number, and they ask, What precise time of day? The intelligence officers tell them the precise time, and the policymakers intercept the truck en route, defuse the bomb, arrest the driver, and then go off for a well-deserved weekend. Then a reporter catches up with the policymaker and asks, What's up? There seems to be a lot of movement out at intelligence headquarters. Oh, nothing much is going on, says the policymaker with a shrug. Those guys are always flapping over something.

It is the same in business. An intelligence outfit gets wind that a competitor will shortly announce a new pricing strategy. It passes word to the chief executive, along with a sufficient amount of information about the market and the company's customers to enable the chief executive and his aides to counter their competitor's impending strategy and leave the other company writhing in the dust. The plan is executed flawlessly; the competitor gets creamed. The chief executive gets his face on the cover of *Business Week.* He orders that bonuses be given to each and every member of—the public relations staff.

Policymakers hate to admit that they acted on good intelligence. They think it diminishes their own competence in someone else's eyes when it becomes known that a seemingly brilliant decision or action was quite obvious because the intelligence was so good no policymaker could have blown it. You should never feel this way. As a policymaker the intelligence outfit belongs to you. Its triumphs are your triumphs. Don't worry about sharing the credit. When something goes right there is glory enough for all. And to an intelligence outfit, a share of the credit for something that goes right is so rare that even the smallest gesture will pay off handsomely in terms of enthusiasm and future performance.

LEARN TO WORK WITH A DIFFERENT SORT OF PERSONALITY

The final and deepest source of tension between policymaking and intelligence is the personality split between policymakers and intelligence officers. They are different breeds of cat entirely. To be sure, there are similarities. Each is intelligent, competent, devoted, and so forth. But the differences are far more striking than the similarities.

A policymaker enjoys power. He likes to make decisions, and to make them fast. He enjoys shifting rapidly from one complex issue to the next. A policymaker relishes the outward trappings of real power. He likes the attention that it brings. When traveling, he likes being met at airports, whisked through customs as a VIP, shuttled from hotel to meeting to dinner in a shiny limousine while escorted by local hosts who fuss and flutter lest the policymaker's slightest whim go begging. It is important to the policymaker that everyone he meets knows precisely who he is. His role, his influence, his power all serve to shape and define his identity. In short, the policymaker is an insider, comfortable only when his own sense of belonging is recognized and accepted by everybody else.

The intelligence officer distrusts power, and therefore

he distrusts those who hold power and visibly enjoy it. The intelligence officer hesitates to make decisions without a total command of all the facts—which, of course, he almost never has. When pressed to act he does so with reluctance, not with relish. When he becomes absorbed in an issue, he becomes totally absorbed. He works, eats, sleeps, breathes, and lives with that issue. He hates to let it go. He wants to stay with the issue long after it has been dealt with for the moment and replaced by some other pressing one.

The intelligence officer is unmoved by the outward trappings of power. Indeed, he is offended by them. He dislikes personal attention, and in general would rather be ignored than singled out publicly, even for praise. When traveling, he prefers to go alone. He actually enjoys arriving in a strange city or country in the middle of the night, waiting his turn to pass through customs, and taking the opportunity to look, to listen, to get a feel for the place and for the people around him. He would rather take a taxi or even a bus to his appointments, and while doing so mingle with the locals. To the intelligence officer, being whisked around in a limousine is like being kept in a plastic bubble; you cannot touch or smell the world around you. To the traveling policymaker, a dinner party canceled at the last minute is a crisis; to the traveling intelligence officer, it is a godsend. At last, he has the opportunity to dress comfortably—anonymously, if you will—and take a long walk to touch, feel, see, hear, and smell the environment. Perhaps he will find a quiet neighborhood restaurant where the real local food may be sampled and where real locals may be quietly observed going about their evening meals. Are they prosperous or poor? Well dressed or sloppy? Quiet or boisterous? Do they talk about politics or private matters? The intelligence officer is essentially a loner, happy spending hours by himself, just watching, learning, thinking, and judging.

A good policymaker is fundamentally a comfortable person. A good intelligence officer is fundamentally an uncomfortable person. To others he often seems to be constantly troubled, petulant, distracted—always in some way dissatisfied with the present state of affairs whatever they may be. Yet these are precisely the qualities that make the intelligence officer so good at what he does. For it is uncomfortable, dissatisfied people who are the most receptive to new ideas and information—who have a knack for spotting trends, seeing patterns amidst the chaos, hearing a melody through all the background noise—who first sense looming change.

Given these personality differences it is a wonder that policymakers and intelligence officers can get along at all. The two tolerate each other; after all they are both professionals. But it doesn't take much of a spark to set off the powder keg.

Keep in mind that intelligence and policymaking *should* be constantly at odds with each other, mutually suspicious and ready to fight at any time. The tension is effective, creative, and healthy. It works. Find an organization whose policymakers and intelligence officers get along too comfortably and you have found yourself an organization in terrible, perhaps even terminal, trouble.

PUT AN INTELLIGENCE CHIEF IN CHARGE

There is one thing that you as a policymaker can do to get the most out of your intelligence outfit and—not coincidentally—to ease the tension between yourself and your policymaking lieutenants on the one hand and your intelligence officers on the other. You can find yourself a good intelligence chief.

Choosing the right person for this job is especially difficult, because managing an intelligence outfit is unlike any other job in government or business. If you think of policymaking and intelligence as two necessary but incompatible systems—rather like two computer mainframes, each built by a different manufacturer—what you need to make them work together is a coupler, a device that sits between the two systems and acts simultaneously as a transmission line and a buffer. This is the role that the chief of an intelligence outfit must play, and it is unique to management; the chief of no other division within any organization plays quite the same role, for there is no other division within government or business whose relationship to policymakers is so sensitive, or so inherently turbulent and volatile. It is a role that very few men and women can play successfully.

An intelligence chief must be able to walk comfortably on both sides of the street. To lead the outfit itself, the chief must have those qualities that mark an intelligence officer: a passion for facts, a taste for delving deeply into issues, an insatiable curiosity about what is really going on in far-off places and about arcane subjects. Yet to work effectively with the chief executive—to understand what the chief executive needs from his intelligence outfit to deliver finished intelligence products in a form the executive can absorb—the intelligence chief must also have the qualities that mark a successful policymaker: a taste for action, the capacity to make decisions when they need to be made, regardless of whether or not all the facts are available, the ruthlessness to accept small losses in pursuit of larger gains.

We are describing a very rare bird indeed. It's an individual who can sit down for lunch in a tent in the middle of a jungle with a group of sweaty insurgents or at a table in a factory canteen with a group of hourly wage workers, or sit down for a state dinner with a bunch of puffed-and-powdered movers-and-shakers, and be equally comfortable and effective in either place. It's an individual who can quite happily wander around a strange city all alone, just to get the feel of it, but who doesn't mind being met at the airport with a red carpet and a limousine to whisk him off to meetings with the local bigwigs. It's an individual who likes the glory that comes with success, but who doesn't need it. In short, it's an individual whom intelligence officers consider one of them, yet whom policymakers also view as among their own.

There are such men and women—not many, but some. Find one and put him or her in charge of your intelligence outfit. Give him or her the responsibility of assuring that you, the policymaker, get whatever you need to know. Make sure it's someone you trust, and make certain that your policymaking lieutenants know you trust this person. Don't let anyone or anything come between yourself and your intelligence chief. Do all these things and you have got yourself one powerful tool for managing. You have vastly increased the chances of your own success.

CHAPTER SIX

THE FUTURE
OF INTELLIGENCE

*What enables the wise sovereign and the good general to
strike and conquer, and achieve things beyond the reach of
ordinary men, is foreknowledge.*

—SUN TZU,
On the Art of War (500 B.C.)

THE spotlight that is beginning to shine on intelligence will continue to shine, and probably grow brighter. The world is not going to become a less complicated place than it is today, nor will the rate of change decrease. If anything, the world will become an even more complicated place in the years and decades that lie before us. And it is likely that the rate of change will quicken. Moreover, the barriers that have fallen to create today's global arena can never be rebuilt. Any country or company that tries to isolate or otherwise box itself off will go belly-up—fast. And, finally, the current torrential flow of information is just a trickle compared with what is ahead.

To lead a large enterprise without access to intelligence will be nothing less than foolhardy. Indeed, as more and more leaders come to recognize that an intelligence outfit is a vital management tool, the current trend toward more carefully structured and thus more effective services and systems will accelerate. In politics, when one government leader makes a point of improving and then relying on his country's intelligence service, that country's foreign adversaries and even allies will feel compelled to do the same. And in business, when one company in a particular industry develops an effective and dynamic intelligence system, it will be hard for the chief executives of competing companies to do nothing in response; their stockholders would scream bloody murder, and rightly so. A perception will very soon take hold that intelligence is like insurance: You cannot afford to be without it no matter how much it costs; and when you need it, it's cheap at the price.

Government intelligence services throughout the world will continue to grow in budgets and personnel. Over time, these services will become more and more sharply focused. That is, they will be organized, and reorganized, and reorganized again until the issues monitored by each intelligence service match precisely those perceived to be vital by the policymakers of that country. Policymakers with accurate perceptions of their country's interests will have at their command a management tool of unique power and precision. They will find it easier to move toward and finally achieve their national objectives. Policymakers with flawed perceptions of their country's interests will come to grief sooner than ever.

In democratic countries like our own, intelligence services will become more visible. As budgets rise, as the number of intelligence officers grows, and as intelligence reports come to play a more regular and central role in policymaking, public attention is sure to follow. This is not necessarily desirable, but it is inevitable. Analytic successes will become widely known, and for the first time policymakers will be publicly judged on how well they use the good intelligence that they receive to chart their country's course. Policymakers who make good use of good intelligence will prosper; policymakers who make bad use of good intelligence will be held to account.

At the same time analytic failures, which happen even to the best services from time to time, will get the notoriety that up to now has been reserved for operational failures. Intelligence analysts will be called to account as never before. They will need to convince the public that they did the best job they could in the time available—that they correctly identified what needed to be known; made their best efforts to collect the raw information; processed that information as fairly and completely as possible; and reached conclusions, judgments, and projections that were sensible, balanced, and free from personal prejudices. If in the event the analysts turned out to be wrong the trick will be to figure out why the mistakes were made, and to avoid these mistakes the next time. With luck the criticism that intelligence analysts receive will be constructive. Alas, politics being what it is we must expect that some of this criticism will be designed to cripple the service itself in hopes of wounding the policymakers. It will be rough out there.

Business intelligence systems will change more dramatically and visibly than their government counterparts. This is simply because they have further to go, and because the secrecy that properly shrouds some parts of government services does not apply in the private sector. Indeed, as the transformation of intelligence from "stealing secrets" to "organized information" continues, business will have more and more running room to plunge ahead.

At most companies, the chief executive will take the first step by asking himself or his lieutenants, What is it we need to know to achieve our objectives? From this point forward, there will be no turning back, for this is one of those rare questions whose very asking begins the process of irrevocable change—one of those questions you can no more ignore than you can unring a bell. It will not be long before the chief executive and his top aides are looking at their company's objectives, and at the plans they have adopted for achieving these objectives, in a new way—namely, with a view toward figuring out precisely what they really need to know to get there. This will be a tough sort of intellectual exercise, but most executives will find that it can also be an invigorating and even exciting one.

With the answer in hand, companies will launch internal "intelligence audits." These audits will be designed to illuminate what information is currently flowing in, from where, and to whom. In every case, the chief executive and his lieutenants will discover that some of what is flowing in is irrelevant, some relevant—and that there is a gap between the total flow in to the company and what its leaders really need.

Filling this gap by creation of intelligence outfits will be the final step. Again, in every case, the chief executive and his lieutenants will discover that some of the various pieces of an intelligence outfit are already in place, however scattered throughout the organization. Hey, what about Joe, who operates out of Brussels and who tracks European technology developments for us? He reports to our research guys, doesn't he? Well, isn't he really gathering intelligence for us? Sure he is. And what about that little economics unit Mary Ann runs, down in the international division? Don't they keep an eye on Japanese trading developments? And don't the guys in marketing do a monthly report on new products that are hitting the market? All this stuff is intelligence, isn't it? Of course it is.

Soon companies will begin to pull it all together. These scattered employees will meet one another—in some cases, quite literally for the first time—and as always happens, a form of synergy will take hold. They will exchange contacts, techniques, ideas, judgments, and so on. In doing so they will deliver to their company an almost instant savings of money and effort. Before long these new informal relationships will become more formally structured. Embryonic intelligence systems will emerge. The whole will prove to be greater than the sum of its parts.

Companies that already have embryonic intelligence outfits in place will expand these outfits. Today most corporate intelligence outfits still focus on "competitor intelligence"—learning what the other guys in the industry are up to. (The answer is always the same: The other guys in the industry are spending precisely the same amount of money, often on the same consultants and sources, trying to learn what you are up to.) Increasingly, this focus on "competitor intelligence" will come to be recognized as too narrow. Like their government counterparts, companies will realize that the proper focus is on the total environment in which the organization must operate; knowing what the competition is up to is useful and perhaps vital, but not sufficient. The winner will be the company with the best grasp of the total environment in which it, and its competitors, are operating.

A BOON FOR STRATEGIC PLANNERS

The growth of existing corporate intelligence outfits, and the emergence of new ones, will be a godsend to strategic planners. For too long now, at far too many companies, these forward-looking staff executives have been shunted aside or even ignored by regular line executives. The line executives' problems are not with the plans themselves, but with the inherent inability of any strategic plan to offer daily, ongoing, real-world guidance to the executive who must implement that plan in an unstable, fast-changing, sometimes even violent commercial environment. As we have seen, intelligence is the crucial but often overlooked second half of strategic planning—the half that enables the planners themselves to make adjustments as real-world trends and events demand.

With access to intelligence, strategic planning will at last be able to fulfill its vital mission. Corporate planning units will become more involved, more operational—more alive—than ever before possible. Creation of a plan will become, as it should be, the first step rather than the last. And the planners themselves, instead of being shunted aside after delivering their basic document, will be in there all the way, where they belong, right in the thick of it. In short, the emergence of corporate intelligence outfits will not displace or even diminish strategic planning. Rather, intelligence will give new life, and in some instances more power, to strategic planning.

Over time, corporate intelligence outfits—again like their government counterparts—will start to show up on organization charts. Of course, there is no one way to build an intelligence outfit into a company. So the structure and location of these outfits will vary. At some companies there will be a chief intelligence officer who reports directly to the chief executive himself. At other companies the intelligence unit will be placed within the strategic planning unit and thus under the direction of the top planning officer. Companies that take a highly decentralized approach to business will build intelligence outfits into each separate division that report to the heads of these divisions, perhaps with one top corporate officer designated to informally watch over the entire network of intelligence units. And some companies will find it most appropriate to name one member of their board of directors to oversee the company's intelligence activities.

In short order we will see the emergence of corporate intelligence specialists. These will be executives who are recognized for their intelligence expertise, as opposed to their financial or marketing expertise. Chief executives who routinely hire executive-search firms will start to hire these headhunters to fill newly created intelligence slots; there will be a growing demand for executives who can fill these slots. Over time, ambitious executives will covet tours of duty in their companies' intelligence systems, just as they now covet tours of duty in the finance and marketing divisions. Intelligence will become one of several recognized routes to the top.

BUYING OUTSIDE INTELLIGENCE

The increased use of business intelligence will fuel the emergence of more intelligence-consulting firms. To be sure, the largest companies will provide most of the intelligence they need internally. But no company can provide for all its needs all the time; besides, having so many experts on so many subjects on the payroll would be too expensive. And with so many consulting firms in the marketplace, it won't be necessary. Most of these firms will remain small and will specialize in providing intelligence on just one or two key subjects. But as the number of these firms increases, the range of subjects they will cover will be enormous—countries, economies, markets, technologies, science, politics, even personalities. For obvious reasons, ex-government officials will continue to be attracted by the idea of launching intelligence-consulting firms—and be attracted by existing firms. As always in the consulting business, the majority of firms will provide a mediocre product. Some will provide a better product and, as always, a few firms will be world-class. In time, the good ones will rise to the top.

The emergence of more and more consulting firms, in turn, will make intelligence available to a wider range of customers. In the short term, it is likely that the largest multinational companies will account for the bulk of these consultants' work. But over time the use of intelligence-consulting firms will spread to smaller companies, especially to those companies striving to expand into foreign markets. Eventually—and the sooner the better—as this new consulting service expands even the smallest start-up business ventures will have access to intelligence at affordable prices. Those entrepreneurs who take advantage of this access will be more likely to survive in the marketplace than those who do not.

All this is good news for both policymakers and intelligence officers. For the officers, in the crassest sense it means better jobs, more pay, and improved working conditions. A certain prestige will attach to intelligence that is not there now. Over time, this will help to attract better people, which, in turn, will boost the pay and prestige of intelligence officers to even higher levels. The trick will be to take these blessings as they come without paying too high a price for them. Who giveth can also taketh away. Intelligence officers will need to resist the temptation to protect their gains by telling policymakers whatever those policymakers want to hear. An intelligence officer who fears losing his job, or his budget, too much to tangle regularly with his policymaking colleagues is worse than a failure; he is a disgrace. He will be giving bad intelligence, and in the end he will lose his budget—and his job—anyway. He will deserve to lose them.

For policymakers, the expansion and refinement of intelligence outfits will provide a powerful tool for managing change. Potential problems will become visible much sooner, thus allowing more time to take evasive action. Potential opportunities will also become visible sooner, allowing time for the sharp, aggressive thrusts that carry a government or company forward along its chosen course. Quite simply, the increased use of intelligence means more chances for success. And you cannot ask for more than that.

Nevertheless, intelligence will always be the trickiest, most annoying, most frustrating, hardest-to-handle management tool. Those of you who choose to use it will need strong stomachs. You will need to endure a steady, accurate monitoring of your own performances. You will be forced to hear—often—why your brilliant and beloved plans are going off the rails. You will need to listen when told of potential problems not currently on your front burners. In short, you will need to recognize that the adversarial relationship between intelligence and policymaking is natural, inevitable, absolutely vital to the success of your enterprise—indeed, to your own personal success. If you don't understand this and accept it, you cannot be a very good policymaker. For you will be operating in a way that puts at risk not only your own career, but the fate of your country or your company.

You were warned at the outset that this book would disclose no secrets. I've changed my mind. Now that I have defined modern intelligence, explained what intelligence outfits do, and shown how intelligence and policymaking fit together, I'm concerned that the effect will be to scare off too many of you. Those of you who are policymakers may conclude that the problems of creating and then managing an intelligence outfit outweigh the potential gains. Budding intelligence officers among you may decide that the financial and professional rewards of this unique business are not worth the headaches that come with it.

So I've decided to spill the one big, closely guarded secret whose disclosure won't land me in jail. It is a secret known to every experienced intelligence officer I have ever met in any country, and to those very few policymakers who use intelligence effectively, but which until now none of these people has ever talked about except among themselves. The secret is this: Intelligence is fun. More than fun, it is interesting, exciting, endlessly fascinating, thoroughly and totally satisfying. When you get the feel of producing good intelligence, or of using good intelligence to achieve your objectives, there is absolutely nothing like it in the world. It is a whole new way of thinking and working.

Leading an enterprise with access to intelligence is like flying into battle at night—but with radar on board. You can see where you are. You can see where you are going. You can see where everybody else is, and where all of them are going. You can avoid surprises, you can sidestep trouble, and when you are ready you can get the drop on your adversaries or competitors. With access to intelligence you have the rarest and most important thing of all to the success of any venture: the confidence and overwhelming sense of safety that comes from seeing clearly enough to figure out precisely what you should do next.